A GIRL'S RIDE IN ICELAND • ALEC-TWEEDIE, MRS. (ETHEL), - 1940

Publisher's Note

Purchase of this book entitles you to a free trial membership in the publisher's book club at www.rarebooksclub.com. (Time limited offer.) Simply enter the barcode number from the back cover onto the membership form on our home page. The book club entitles you to select from millions of books at no additional charge. You can also download a digital copy of this and related books to read on the go. Simply enter the title or subject onto the search form to find them.

Note: This is an historic book. Pages numbers, where present in the text, refer to the first edition of the book and may also be in indexes.

If you have any questions, could you please be so kind as to consult our Frequently Asked Questions page at www.rarebooksclub.com/faqs.cfm? You are also welcome to contact us there.

Publisher: General Books LLC™, Memphis, TN, USA, 2012. ISBN: 9781153794732.

Proofreading: pgdp.net

A GIRL'S RIDE IN ICELAND.

.... 0
.... 0

MRS. ALEC TWEEDIE.
After a painting by Herbert Schmalz.
p. i
A GIRL'S
  RIDE IN ICELAND
  BY
  MRS. ALEC TWEEDIE
  (*Née* HARLEY).
  AUTHOR OF "A WINTER JAUNT TO NORWAY," WITH PERSONAL
    ACCOUNTS OF NANSEN, IB-

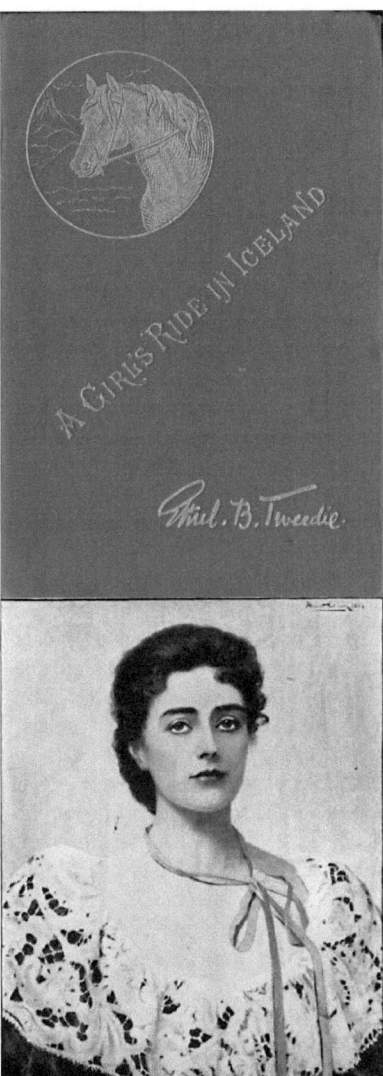

SEN, BJÖRNSEN, AND BRANDES;
  "THE OBERAMMERGAU PASSION PLAY," ETC.

'Iceland shone with glorious lore renowned,
A northern light when all was gloom around.
  Montgomery.
WITH NUMEROUS ILLUSTRATIONS AND A MAP.
  SECOND EDITION.

LONDON: HORACE COX, WINDSOR HOUSE,
BREAM'S BUILDINGS, E.C.
1894.
p. ii
The Rights of Translation and Reproduction are reserved.
p. iii

PREFACE TO THE SECOND EDITION

When this little volume (my maiden effort) was published five years ago, it unwittingly originated an angry controversy by raising the question "Should women ride astride?"

It is astonishing what a great fire a mere spark may kindle, and accordingly the war, on what proved to be a very vexed subject, waged fast and furious. The picture papers inserted cleverly-illustrated articles *pro.* and *con.*; the peace of families was temporarily wrecked, for people were of course divided in their opinions, and bitter things were said by both sides concerning a very simple and harmless matter. For a time it seemed as though the "Ayes" would win; but eventually appearances carried the day, and women still use side saddles when on horseback, though the knickerbockers and short skirts (only far shorter) I advocated for rough country riding are now constantly worn by the many female equestrians who within the last couple of years have mounted bicycles. p. iv

It is nearly four years since, from an hotel window in Copenhagen, I saw, to my great surprise, for the first time a woman astride a bicycle! How strange it seemed! Paris quickly followed suit, and now there is a perfect army of women bicyclists in that fair capital; after a decent show of hesitation England dropped her prejudices, and at the present minute, clad in unnecessarily masculine costume, almost without a murmur, allows her daughters to scour the country in quest of fresh air astride a bicycle.

If women may ride an iron steed thus attired, surely they might be permitted to bestride a horse in like manner clothed, and in like fashion.

In past times women have ridden in every possible position, and in every possible costume. They have ridden sideways on both the near and off sides, they have ridden astride (as the Mexicans, Indians, Tartars, Roumanians, Icelanders, &c., do to-day), and they have also ridden pillion. Queen Elizabeth rode thus behind the Earl of Leicester on public occasions, in a full hoop skirt, low-necked bodice, and large ruffs. Nevertheless, she dispensed with a cavalier when out hunting, at the ripe age of seventy-six.

When hunting, hawking, or at tournaments, women in the middle ages always rode astride in this country, reserving their side saddles merely for state functions. Judging from old pictures, they then mounted arrayed in full ball dresses, in long-veiled headdresses (time of p. v Edward II.), and in flowing skirts, while their heads were often ornamented with huge plumed hats.

Formerly, every church door, every roadside inn, had its horse block or "jumping-on stone"—called in Kent and some other southern counties the "joist stone," and in Scotland the "louping-on stane." These were necessary in the olden days of heavy armour, and at a time when women rode astride. Men can now mount alone, although the struggles of a small man to climb to the top of a big horse sometimes are mightily entertaining; but women have to trust to any capable or incapable man who can assist them into their saddles.

Fashion is ephemeral. Taste and public opinion having no corporal identity, are nothing but the passing fancy of a given generation.

Dress to a woman always seems an important matter, and to be well dressed it is necessary to be suitably clothed. Of course breeches, high boots or leggings are essential in riding; but a neatly arranged divided skirt, reaching well below the knee, can be worn over these articles, and the effect produced is anything but inelegant. Of one thing we may be certain, namely, that whenever English women summon up enough courage to ride their horses man fashion again, every London tailor will immediately set himself to design becoming and useful divided skirts for the purpose.

I strongly advocate the abolition of the side saddle for the country, hunting, or rough journeys, p. vi for three reasons—1st, safety; 2nd, comfort; 3rd, health.

I. Of course nothing is easier under ordinary circumstances than to "stick on" a side saddle, because the pommels almost hold one there: herein lies much danger. In the case of a horse falling, for instance, a woman (although doubtless helped by the tight skirts of the day) cannot extricate herself. She is caught in the pommels or entangled by the stirrups, both of which calamities mean dragging, and often result in a horrible death.

II. Miss Bird, in her famous book of travels, tells us how terribly her back suffered from hard riding on a side-saddle, and how easily she accomplished the same distances when, disregarding conventionalities, she adopted a man's seat.

The wife of a well-known Consul-General, who, in company with her husband, rode in similar fashion from Shanghai to St. Petersburgh through Siberia, always declared such a feat would have been impossible for her to achieve on a side-saddle. Further, the native women of almost all countries ride astride to this day, as they did in England in the fourteenth century.

My own experience as to comfort will be found in the following pages, and I can only add that greater knowledge has strengthened my opinion.

III. Cross riding has been considered injurious to health by a few members of the medical profession, but the majority hold a different opinion. p. vii

When discussing the subject with Sir John Williams—one of the greatest authorities on the diseases of women—he said, "I do not see that any harm could arise from women riding like men. Far from it. I cannot indeed conceive why the side saddle was ever invented at all. " What more could be urged in favour of cross riding.

Do we not all know that many girls become crooked when learning to ride, and have to mount on the off side in order to counteract the mischief. Is this not proof in itself of how unnatural the position must be?

As women ride at the present moment, horses with sore backs are unfortunately no rarity. It is true these galls are caused by bad riding; still, such things would be avoided with a man's saddle, which is far lighter than a woman's, and easier to carry, because the rider's weight is not on one side, but equally distributed—a great comfort to the horse's loins and withers.

We all know that a woman's horse is far sooner knocked up with a hard day than one ridden by a man, although the man is probably the heavier weight of the two, and this merely because he is properly balanced.

Since this little book made its first appearance, many ladies have followed the advice therein contained, and visited "the most volcanic region of the earth," peeped at Iceland's snow-clad peaks and deeply indented fjords, made acquaintance with its primitive people, and ridden their shaggy ponies. p. viii Practically Iceland remains the same today as it was a century ago. Time passes unheeded within its borders, and a visit to the country is like returning to the Middle Ages. Excepting in the capital, to all intents and purposes, no change is to be noted; and even there the main square opposite the governor's house forms the chief cod-fish drying-ground, while every summer the same odours ascend from the process as greeted travellers of yore.

Thanks, however, to the courtesy of a couple of friends, I am able to mention a few innovations. Dr. Karl Grossman, who travelled through the north-west of the island, on geology intent, has kindly furnished me with excellent photographs of ponies.

Mr. T. J. Jeaffreson, who knows the island well, intends before joining Mr.

Frederick Jackson's polar expedition, to explore and cross the interior of Iceland from east to west during the winter of 1894-95, on or about the 68th parallel, traversing the practically unknown districts of Storis-anch, Spengis-andr, and O-dadahraimm, and returning across the Vatna Jokull or Great Ice Desert. His reasons for wishing to cross in the winter are, first, that in summer ponies must be used for the journey, and they could not carry sufficient food and fuel for the expedition as well as fodder for themselves; second, the roughness of the ground and the weight of the burdens would necessitate very short distances being traversed each day.

Mr. Jeaffreson will, as did Dr. Nansen when he p. ix crossed Greenland, use ski and Canadian snow-shoes, and drag his own sledges, in preference to using ponies or dogs. We may look for an interesting volume on the natural history of Iceland from his pen.

Some slight but desirable improvements have been effected in the Capital Reykjavik, the most important being the erection of quite a nice little hotel "Iseland," which is kept by Halburg, who speaks excellent English, and whose son, formerly a waiter in this country, is a good sportsman and guide. Ponies are supplied at this hotel.

The chief guide in Iceland is now Thorgrimmer Goodmanson. He speaks several languages fluently, and is by profession the English and Latin schoolmaster; during the summer months, nevertheless, he acts as guide.

The museum has been much enlarged, and is now located in the House of Parliament.

There is a new hospital, and very good public washing sheds have been erected for the town at the hot springs about a mile distant.

There are now several shops, perhaps a dozen, and among them an excellent sporting outfitters, where English cartridges and salmon flies can be procured.

Most of the pony track from Meijkjavik to Akureyri has been marked by stone cairns which show black against the winter's snow; and as there is now a post for nine months of the year (the boats running occasionally in the winter), letters p. x are carried on horseback across from the capital to Akureyri every four weeks.

The "Camöens" runs no longer, but the Danish boats stop at Leith once a fortnight (excepting during January, February, and March, when the island is ice-bound), and after calling at three places in the Faroës and at Westmann Islands (weather permitting) go straight to Reykjavik.

The road from the capital to the Geysers is as rough as ever, but at Thingvalla Parsonage two or three little cabin bed-rooms have been put up, beds being very preferable to the floor in the opinion of weary travellers.

Tents are still necessary at the Geysers, although a two-roomed shed is in process of erection for the accommodation of visitors.

The Stroker Geyser, which stopped for some time, is now working again, and is kept covered with a little lattice wood lid.

Mr. Jeaffreson told me that at Yellowstone Park, in America, visitors are carefully watched to see that they do not make the geysers work artificially by means of soap. (Hardly explicable in such small quantities by chemistry or physics.) Remembering this experience the last time he went to Iceland, he packed some 2lb. bars of common soap among his luggage.

"When I got to the Geysers," he continued, "the dirty old Icelander guarding them asked me for 5 kroner to make the Stroker play. When I p. xi refused his request he became most abusive, but, seeing I was inexorable, finally went away, declaring the geyser would never play unless I paid him, and I declaring as emphatically that it would, and directly too.

"As soon as he was at a safe distance I looked up my bars of soap, and dropping a couple of them under the lid, awaited the result. Very shortly a hiss and a groan were heard, and up went the boiling water, sending the wooden grating into the air.

"Back rushed the dirty man, not knowing whether to abuse or worship me as a worker of miracles. He was profoundly impressed, and finally declared he had never seen Stroker play so well before, but—— 'Was it the Devil who had worked the game?'

"I had not enough soap left to try the big geyser, so waited a couple of days to see it play. Fortunately it did so in the end."

If the story of Stroker spread, which it is sure to do in such a very superstitious country, Mr. Jeaffreson will be regarded with a certain amount of awe when he starts on his ski (snow-shoes) expedition next winter.

Although his proposed trip is somewhat dangerous, I hope he may return as happily as Dr. Nansen did from Greenland, and extract as much pleasure out of his skilöbning as we contrived to do by visiting Norway when that glorious land was covered with snow and bound by ice. p. xii

When I pen these last lines, on July 12, 1894, I have just returned from seeing Frederick Jackson and his gallant followers steam away down Thames in their quest of the North Pole. A party of friends and several leading Arctic explorers assembled at Cannon-street Station this morning to see the English Polar Expedition off. Five minutes before the train left, Frederick Jackson, who having discarded the frock coat and top hat which had earned for him the reputation of "resembling a smart guardsman with handsome bronzed features," appeared upon the scene with his favourite brother. To-day the leader of the expedition looked like an English yachtsman in blue serge; but he did not personally provoke so much comment as his luggage. All the heavy things were already on board the "Windward," anchored off Greenhithe. When the hero of the hour arrived, a large Inverness cape on his arm, carrying a bundle of fur rugs, his only article of luggage was a large tin bath!

"A bath," we cried.

"Yes," he laughingly replied, "I've had a small bath-room built on the ship, and when we get into our winter quarters on Bell Island I shall use my 'baby's bath.' I can rough it, and I have roughed it for years, but there is one thing I can't go without—a good tub."

What a true Englishman!

Frederick Jackson was in the best of spirits, and never gave way for a moment, although those many, many goodbyes exchanged with intimate p. xiii friends must have been a sore trial. In spite of his tremendous self-control, he is strangely tenderhearted and affectionate by nature.

When we reached Greenhithe it was raining; but the boats from the "Worcester," manned by smart lads, were waiting for us, and with hard pulling—for the tide was running fast—we were all soon clambering up a rope ladder to the "Windward's" decks. There was not much room. Food at full rations (6½ lb. per man per diem) for eight men for four years fills a good space, and five or six tons of cod liver oil biscuits for the dogs, twelve tons of compressed hay for the ponies, sledges, tents, boats, clothing, &c., was more than the hold could accommodate, and some of the things strewed the deck.

There was considerable fun getting the shaggy black retrievers on board, for they could not walk up a rope ladder, and were almost too big to carry.

Just as we were all leaving to go on board the "Worcester" and watch the final start, it was discovered that one of the picked eight of the land party had never turned up!

Had he lost heart, or made a mistake as to the time of departure?

Great was the consternation, and eagerly all eyes were turned to the shore; but still he came not. As it afterwards transpired, he had missed his train; and, far from his courage having failed at the last moment, so eager was he to be off, he travelled on to Gravesend, where, thanks to the courtesy of an official of high rank, he was put on board a gunboat, p. xiv and raced down the Thames, just managing to get alongside the Arctic ship before it was too late.

From H.M.S. "Worcester" we watched the anchor weighed, and as the boys manned the rigging of the two training ships, they sent up a tremendous roar of cheers. Flags were flying on every side, for several yachts had come to see the start. "God Save the Queen" sounded across the water from the land, and the sun came out and shone brightly as the stout whaler "Windward" steamed away with her party of Polar explorers in the best of spirits.

A couple of months hence they will be settling down in their winter quarters in Franz Josef Land, there to wait through the Arctic darkness for the return of the sun, when they will push on towards the North Pole, leaving a chain of depôts behind them.

Everyone must wish them "God speed."

They may meet Dr. Nansen, and Mr. Jackson was immensely amused when I handed him a letter for my good friend—addressed

Dr. Fridtjof Nansen,
North Pole .

Kindly favoured by F. G. Jackson.

How strange it will be if these two adventurous men really meet and shake hands beneath the Polar star! May good fortune attend them, and their enthusiasm be rewarded.

E. B. T.
London , *12th July, 1894.*

LIST OF ILLUSTRATIONS.

		PAGE
PORTRAIT OF AUTHOR	(Frontispiece) Herbert Schmalz	1 1
FIRST VIEW OF ICELAND	Author	28 .. 1
AKUREYRI	Dr. Grossman (photograph)	32 .. 1
NATIVE WOMAN	Herbert Schmalz	34 .. 1
THE FERRY	Dr. Grossman	37 .. 1
PONIES FORDING RIVER	"	63 .. 1
OUR MODE OF RIDING	G. D. Giles	66 .. 1
ICELANDIC FARM	Author	74 .. 1
DRANGEY FROM REYKIR	"	79 .. 1
HRUTA FJORD AND FARM	"	86 .. 1
SNAEFELL JÖKULL	"	90 .. 1
REYKJAVIK	F. P. Fellows	91 .. 1
THINGVALLA PARSONAGE	Author	114
PONIES CROSSING LAKE	Dr. Grossman	117
STROKER IN ERUPTION	Author	122
NATIVE IMPLEMENTS	"	132
DIAGRAM OF GEYSERS	George Harley, F.R.S.	164
MAP OF ICELAND.		

PAGE
CHAPTER I.
Our Start —Description of Party—Messrs R. & D. Slimon, of Leith—Kit and Provisions—Slimon's Ticket Office—Non-Arrival of One of the Party—Final Preparations, 1
CHAPTER II.
Under Weigh —Price of Tickets—Crew and General Accommodation—Rough Weather—Shelter in Sinclair Bay—Letters taken off by Fishing Smack—Fellow Passengers—Sight First Whale—John o' Groat's House, 12
CHAPTER III.
Land Sighted —Man Overboard—His Recovery described—Iceland Sighted—Temperature and Position of the Island—Anchored off Akureyri—Icelandic Boat—Male and Female Costumes, 24
CHAPTER IV.
Akureyri —Pack Ponies—No Wheeled Conveyances— 37

Woman's Saddle—House Interior—Staple Food—Absence of Domestic Animals and Timber—An Akureyri Dinner—Constitution of the Reykjavik Bank—Icelandic and English Money Table—Gléra Waterfall—Frost Mounds—Shark Oil Manufactory—Native Artist and Poet—Establishment of an Icelandic College,

CHAPTER V.

Historical Notes —Early History of Iceland—Population—Commonwealth Established—Conquest of the Isle of Man—Tynwald Hill—Chronological Dates—A Curious Custom—Landing of First Christian Missionary—Roman Catholicism embraced—Annexation to Norway—Area of the Island—Its Lakes and Rivers, 52

CHAPTER VI.

Sauderkrok —An Auction—Imports and Exports—Experience in Riding a Man's Saddle—Costume—Sketching—Curiosity of the Natives—Ride to Reykir—Hot Springs—A Young Student—Literature and Language—The Sagas, 63

CHAPTER VII.

Reykir —A Farm House—Skyr—Hot Springs utilised for Washing purposes—A Legend—The Eider Duck—Hay—Icelandic Flora—Bordeyri—Curious Form of Hospitality—Emigrants—12th August—Within the Arctic Circle, 75

CHAPTER VIII.

Reykjavik —Preparations for Visiting the Geysers—Principal Buildings—Founding of the Town by 'Tugolfi'—A Primitive Newspaper—Start for the Geysers—Professor Geikie on Icelandic Volcanoes—Eruptions—Skaptar-Jökull—Lunch in the Valley of the Seljadalr—Thingvalla Lake—The Almannagya, 92

CHAPTER IX.

Thingvalla —Site of the First Icelandic Parliament—The Althing—Conversion to Christianity—Abolition of the Althing—New Constitution of 1874—Thingvalla Parsonage—Antique Grinding Machine—A Tintron—Dust Storm—Hot Springs—Arrival at the Geysers, 107

CHAPTER X.

The Geysers —Tents blown down—The Great Geyser—Eruption of the 'Stroker'—Professor Geikie and Dr Kneeland on Geysers—Dinner—A Night in a Tent—Hot Springs of the District—Hecla in the Distance—Farewell to the Geysers, 121

CHAPTER XI.

Farm House —An Icelandic Dairy—Farm Kitchen—A Family Bedroom—Bruara Bridge—Back to Reykjavik—Population—The Great Awk—Leave Iceland—Northern Lights—Land at Granton—Table of Expenditure, 133

CHAPTER XII.

Volcanoes —The Askja Volcano—Large Fissure in Midge Lake Desert—Krafla—Skaptar-Jökull—Great Eruption of 1783—Hecla—Thermal Springs—The Usahver, 147

APPENDIX.

' Geysers '—Dr George Harley, F.R.S., 157

p. 1

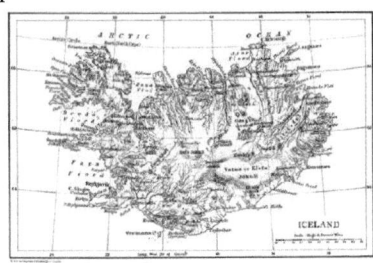

ICELAND

A GIRL'S RIDE IN ICELAND.

CHAPTER I.

OUR START.

As the London season, with its thousand and one engagements, that one tries to cram into the shortest possible time, draws to a close, the question uppermost in every one's mind is, 'Where shall we go this autumn?' And a list of places well trodden by tourists pass through the brain in rapid succession, each in turn rejected as too far, too near, too well known, or not embracing a sufficient change of scene.

Switzerland? Every one goes to Switzerland: that is no rest, for one meets half London there. Germany? The same answer occurs, and so on *ad infinitum*.

'Suppose we make up a party and visit Iceland?' was suggested by me to one of my friends on a p. 2 hot July day as we sat chatting together discussing this weighty question, fanning ourselves meanwhile under a temperature of ninety degrees; the position of Iceland, with its snow-capped hills and cool temperature seeming positively refreshing and desirable. Mad as the idea seemed when first proposed in mere banter, it ended, as these pages will prove, by our turning the suggestion into a reality, and overcoming the difficulties of a trip which will ever remain engraven on my memory as one of the most agreeable experiences of my life.

When I ventilated the idea outside my private 'den,' wherein it first arose, it was treated as far too wild a scheme for serious consideration—for 'Iceland,' to Londoners, seems much the same in point of compass as the moon! And there really is some similarity in the volcanic surface of both. Here, however, the similarity ends, for while the luminary is indeed inaccessible, the island can easily be reached without any very insurmountable difficulty.

The somewhat natural opposition which our plan at first met with, only stimulated our desire the more to carry it into effect. The first step was to gain the permission of our parents, which, after some reluctance, was granted, and the necessary ways and means finally voted; our next was to collect together a suitable party from our numerous friends, and take all necessary measures to secure the success of the undertaking. p. 3

As soon as our purpose became known and discussed among our immediate circle of friends, many volunteers appeared anxious to share the triumphs of so novel an enterprise.

Thus our number at first promised to be somewhat larger than we had anticipated. Happily, however, for its success, as it afterwards proved, these aspirants for 'fame,' on learning the length of the passage, the possible discomforts, and other obstacles, dropped off one by one, till only my brother and myself, with three other friends, remained firm to our purpose.

It may be well here to introduce our party individually to my readers.

First, my brother, whom, for convenience sake in these pages, I will call by his Christian name, 'Vaughan,' and whom I looked upon as the head of the expedition, as, without his protection, I should never have been allowed to undertake the trip.

He was a medical student in Edinburgh (since fully qualified), and well suited to the enterprise, being of a scientific turn of mind, as well as practical and energetic,—a first-rate rider, an oarsman, and a good sailor, whilst he had spent his vacations for some years in travelling.

My friend Miss T., my sole lady companion, a handsome girl of a thoroughly good-natured and enterprising disposition, was, on the contrary, no horsewoman, but the exigencies of a trip in Iceland soon made her one. She was an excellent German scholar, and a great assistance to our party in this p. 4 respect, as the natives could often understand German, from the resemblance of that language to Danish.

As it proved afterwards, it was really fortunate that we had not more than two ladies in our party, for a larger number could hardly have met with the necessary accommodation. Ladies are such rare visitors in Iceland, that little or no preparation is made for their comfort. The captain of our vessel told us that during several voyages last year he had not a single female passenger on board.

H. K. Gordon, an Anglo-Indian, on leave from Calcutta for his health, was likewise a valuable addition to our number. He was accustomed to tent life and camping out, and helped us much in similar experiences.

A. L. T., who completed our party, was a keen sportsman, but the novelties of the trip overbalanced his love for Scotland and the attractions of the 12th of August—no small sacrifice, especially as our travelling proved too rapid to enable him to make much use of his gun, although we often saw game in our various rides.

Of myself, I have only to say that, being worn out with the gaieties of a London season, I looked forward to a trip to 'Ultima Thule' with pleasurable anticipations, which were ultimately fully realised.

Five is not a bad number to form a travelling company, and a very happy five we were, although entirely thrown on our own resources for twenty p. 5 five days. Of course we were often placed in the queerest positions, over which we laughed heartily; for on starting we agreed that we would each and all make the best of whatever obstacles we might encounter, and it is certainly no use going to Iceland, or any other out-of-the-way place, if one cannot cheerfully endure the absence of accustomed luxuries. Travellers not prepared to do this had better remain at home.

The decision once arrived at that Iceland was to be our Autumn destination, we endeavoured to collect from our travelling friends any information on the subject, either as regarded route, outfit, or mode of travelling, and whether the scenery and novelty of the trip were likely to repay us for the trouble and roughing we should have to undergo; but unfortunately all our investigations were futile, as we found no one who had any personal knowledge of the Island. I, however, remembered Dr John Rae, the famous discoverer of the Franklin remains, was an old friend of my father's, and therefore wrote to ask him if he could help us in our difficulties, but his answer was not of a cheering nature, as he had not been in the Island for twenty-five years, and he had then only crossed from east to west—from Bevufjord to Kekiaviati, which did not form part of our route. He further stated he thought it was too arduous an undertaking for ladies, and dissuaded us from making the attempt. Failing to obtain any assistance from such a high authority, we concluded that it would be useless p. 6 to make any further inquiries among our personal friends; we were therefore compelled to rely upon our own resources, and extract what information we could from guide books. Our inquiry at a London ticket office whether the officials could give us any particulars as to our route, was equally unsuccessful, the astonished clerk remarking,—'I was once asked for a ticket to the North Pole, but I have never been asked for one to Iceland.'

But although we never procured any personal experiences, we found there was no lack of interesting historical and geological literature respecting the Island.

Our first step was to place ourselves in communication with Messrs R. D. Slimon, of Leith, the managers of the Icelandic Steamship Company, from whom we learnt that the next steamer would start from Leith on the 31st July (such, at least, was the advertised time and place), but it really left Granton, some three miles further up the Forth, an hour and a half later than was originally fixed.

Before proceeding any further, it may be well to mention the important subjects of outfit and provisions. As we were not going upon a fashionable tour, it was not necessary to provide ourselves with anything but what was really needed. Intending travellers must recollect that, as all inland journeys are performed on ponies, and the luggage can only be slung across the animals' backs, large boxes or trunks are out of the question, and it is necessary to compress one's outfit into the smallest p. 7 possible dimensions. The following list will be found quite sufficient for the journey.

A thick serge dress, short and plain for rough wear, with a cloth one in change; a tight-fitting thick jacket, good mackintosh, and very warm fur cloak; one pair of high mackintosh riding boots (like fisherman's waders), necessary for crossing rivers and streams; a yachting cap or small tight-fitting hat, with a projecting peak to protect the eyes from the glare—blue glasses, which are a great comfort; thick gauntlet gloves; a habit skirt is not necessary.

My brother has given me a list of things he found most useful. Two rough homespun or serge suits: riding breeches, which are absolutely indispensable; riding boots laced up the centre, and large, as they are continually getting wet; flannel shirts; thick worsted stockings; a warm ulster, and mackintosh.

Instead of trusting to the pack boxes provided by the natives, a soft waterproof 'hold-all,' or mule boxes, would be an additional comfort.

On one of our long rides, two pack ponies came into collision, they both fell, the path being very narrow, and rolled over one another. To our horror, one pack box was broken to pieces, while another lost its bottom, and there in all the dust lay tooth brushes, sponge bags, etc., not to mention other necessaries of the toilet.

Rugs, mackintosh sheets, and pillows are required for camping out, also towels. Although the p. 8 Icelanders provide tents, it is advisable to take your own if feasible. Provisions are absolutely requisite—tinned meats and soup, and a cooked ham or tongues; tea, sugar, cocoa, biscuits (of a hard make), and as no white bread is to be procured, it is as well to induce the ship's steward to provide some loaves before starting on an expedition. Butter can be obtained at Reikjavik. Japanned plates and mugs, knives, forks, and spoons, must not be forgotten. We provided ourselves with wine and spirits, which we found of great use to face the cold.

Our purchases being made and our party complete, we arranged to start from Euston on Thursday, 29th July, and go north by the night train. My brother, however, was to meet us at Edinburgh, as he had been away in his small yacht, coasting near Dunbar. We had, however, sent him all particulars as to our plans. Under the best circumstances, and despite sleeping saloons, and other luxuries, it is a long and tedious journey to Scotland, and we were not sorry to find it at an end, as, with a puff and a shriek, our train entered the Waverley Station, Edinburgh.

Notwithstanding our fatigue, we took a somewhat regretful look at that steam marvel of civilisation, which had brought us thus far on our journey, and to which we now bade farewell for a month, at least, for a much ruder and more primitive mode of travelling.

Some friends had kindly offered to put us up p. 9 during our short stay, so we made our way to their house, and were soon enjoying the luxuries of a wash and a good breakfast. My brother had arranged to meet us there, but as he did not put in an appearance, we determined to go in search of him at his rooms.

Imagine our dismay on arriving there to be told by his landlady that he had been absent for a week, yachting, and had not yet returned, whilst all our letters detailing our final plans, and date of arrival in Edinburgh, were lying unopened on the table.

We at once determined to take energetic measures to discover any tidings of his whereabouts. As it was necessary to go to Leith to engage cabins and take tickets, we decided to push on to Granton, where I knew he kept his boat, and inquire at the Royal Forth Yacht Club if they knew anything about *The Lily* and her owner.

A tram car took Miss T. and myself to Leith, and after sundry inquiries, we found ourselves in front of an ordinary tin-shop, over which the name 'Slimon' was painted in large letters of gold—an unlikely-looking place, we thought, to take tickets for such an important voyage.

In answer to our inquiries, 'Yes, mum, the office is next door,' was vouchsafed to us in the broadest Scotch dialect, by a clerk, who escorted us there, carrying with him a huge bunch of keys, looking more like a gaoler conducting prisoners, than two p. 10 ladies innocently requiring tickets. We were ushered into a dingy little office, where we found the only occupant was a cat! Our conductor was extremely ignorant, and unable to supply us with any information, his answer to every question being, 'I dinna ken,' or 'I canna say.'

I explained to him what anxiety I was in about my missing brother, and that our party would have to be broken up unless he appeared before the morrow; consequently, it would be useless for us to purchase tickets until we heard from him. He blurted out in a broad and almost unintelligible dialect, which I am unable to reproduce, that we need not pay until we were on board the steamer, adding, that probably the dead calm since the previous night had delayed *The Lily*. I knew Vaughan had intended going out beyond Dunbar, and feared that he might be out in a gale; but if only becalmed, I felt certain he would somehow manage to get ashore in the dinghy, and was confident he had ascertained for himself, independently of our unopened letters, the date of the steamer's starting, and was too old a traveller to fail his party, and so spoil the expedition *in toto*.

Rattling over the stones to Granton in a terribly rickety 'machine,' as our northern friends call their cabs, the first old salt we encountered on the pier replied to our anxious inquiry, 'Why, that's *The Lily* sailing round the harbour's mouth,' as at that moment she slowly rounded the pier.

When Vaughan came ashore, he told us, after p. 11 running from Dunbar in a gale, he had been becalmed for two days, and it had taken the whole of that day to cross 'the Forth.' He had not hurried particularly, however, thinking we were not travelling North till the next day, no letters having been forwarded to him. Thus ended happily what might have been a great catastrophe, and compelled us to abandon the expedition.

That night we returned with him to Edinburgh, and on rising next morning from probably the last comfortable bed we should enjoy for some time, we were cheered by a bright sun and cloudless sky—a pleasant forecast for the voyage in prospect. We made several purchases in Princes Street, inclusive of an extra deck chair, warm rugs, etc., and received an influx of '*bon voyage*' telegrams from our London friends—the last home news we should get for a month. Yes, four weeks is a long time never to hear of one's nearest and dearest, or they to hear of you. What might not happen in the interval? So much, indeed, that it passes contemplation, and we had best leave it, and content ourselves with the fact that we had left every one well, and everything all right when we started.

At the pier we found the tender waiting to take us to the *Camoens*, the steamer which was to convey us to the goal of our ambition, namely, Iceland.

How many and varied were our experiences before we steamed alongside that pier again! p. 12

CHAPTER II.

UNDER WEIGH.

The *Camoens*, named after the Portuguese poet of that name, is a fair-sized steamer of 1200 tons, which runs during the summer and autumn months at regular intervals of about once in four weeks, between Granton and Reikjavik, the capital of Iceland, calling *en route* at other ports. Subjoined is a map of the Island, with a red boundary line marking the course of the steamer, and her usual halting places.

Her average run, inclusive of stoppage at the various trading ports, is six or seven days at most; but in steaming direct from Granton to the Icelandic capital, the voyage does not occupy more than three and a half days, if the weather is favourable.

On reaching the *Camoens*, we found the rest of our party already arrived, and we joined forces at once. All was not ready, however, on board, for the stowage of the cargo was still in full swing, and sacks of flour and trusses of hay were being alternately hurled round on the crane and lowered on deck, sailors and 'odd hands' rushing hither and thither in the wildest confusion. p. 13

Just before our arrival a serious accident had occurred. The steward was returning from market, when the crane struck him and knocked him down, injuring the poor man sadly, breaking both his arms, and causing severe contusions of the head. He was carried ashore to the hospital, and but slight hopes were entertained of his recovery.

This fatality caused the greatest inconvenience, for independent of his being a valuable steward, and the sorrow to his messmates at his accident, it is not generally easy, just as a steamer is leaving port, to find a substitute. Happily, in this case, a former steward being disengaged, the captain at once secured his services; but as he only came on board at the last moment, and neither knew where the supplies were stored, nor of what they consisted, the ship's company was thereby put to much inconvenience during the voyage.

Messrs Slimons' agent was on board the *Camoens* with his ticket book, and our tickets were at once procured; not expensive by any means, being only £8 each person to Iceland and back, including the trip round the Island; our food being charged at the rate of 6s. 6d. per day extra.

The best berth cabin had been reserved for Miss T. and myself, the one opposite for the three gentlemen, with an intermediate passage, which latter proved a great comfort, as it contained hooks for coats and cloaks, and room for two portmanteaus.

The cabins were unusually small, and required p. 14 very close arrangement of our effects, and the extra hooks and cabin bags for the wall we had brought with us were most useful.

Our crew numbered thirty-two in all, and rough-looking specimens of humanity they indeed appeared. We had two stewardesses, who also waited at table, and made themselves generally useful. These were slatternly in appearance, but were very attentive and kind-hearted. There were seven firemen, two working at the same time for four hours at a stretch, thus each couple did duty twice in the twenty-four hours; which means eight hours in the engine-room out of the twenty-four.

There were forty berths on board the *Camoens*, only nineteen of which were occupied during the outward voyage. The ship carried no surgeon, consequently my brother was frequently applied to in cases of burns, sprains, etc.

The captain had a large Board of Trade medicine chest, of which he kept the key, and from which he usually administered the contents when required, to the best of his medical knowledge. I must here refer with ready praise to the kindness of Captain Robertson, a most worthy man, and of general information. He often came and sat with us in the evening in the saloon, or smoked with the gentlemen, and many and varied were the yarns he spun.

We got under weigh about 4.30 on Saturday afternoon, July 31st, being tugged out of the p. 15 harbour at Granton. The Firth of Forth was then as calm as a lake, scarce a ripple to be seen on its surface. A previous thunderstorm had freshened the air, the rain which had fallen had ceased, and those lovely mists and tints usually to be seen after a storm, had taken the place of the dark clouds now rolling away in the distance. Inchkeith was spanned by a lovely rainbow, and peace, quiet, and beauty reigned around. The water, indeed, was more like a large lake, such as the 'Chiem See' in Bavaria—dotted with its islands—than an inlet of the sea.

On we steamed, passing Leith, Portobello, North Berwick, with the Bass Rock and the coast of Fife, and, as evening drew on, May Island and Bell Rock. It was indeed a lovely night. The sky, lit up with the deep, warm glow of the departing sun, cast a rosy hue over the whole expanse of water. A night, indeed, so perfect, we all agreed it was worth coming to sea to witness and enjoy.

The human mind is, however, versatile, and before morning we had cause to change our ideas, and several of us already wished ourselves again at home!

On entering the Moray Firth the evening calm of the untroubled sea was exchanged for rough billows, and hour by hour we became more and more miserable, each alike in turn paying our tribute to Neptune, and truly realising the differ p. 16 ence between a voyage in prospect and one in stern reality.

My brother, Mr Gordon, the captain, and two other passengers were the sole occupants of the saloon at breakfast. At luncheon, the latter couple were also absent, and more people than ourselves bewailed their misery, and wished themselves back ashore.

The rolling of the steamer was tremendous. It pitched and tossed to such an extent that our bags and other things in our cabin were tumbled about in every direction. Despite the discomfort, we struggled on deck about twelve o'clock, hoping the air would revive us, and in half an hour felt quite other persons.

The worst of a rough sea is, that when one is feeling sick, and air is most needed, one is obliged to shut the portholes, and only imbibe that which comes from the saloon—a mixture of fumes by no means invigorating.

I had always prided myself on being a good sailor when on yachting excursions and short sea voyages, but that 'Moray Firth' undeceived me in this respect. My misery, however, soon wore off, and save on this occasion, and one day on our return voyage, even in the rough days we encountered in the Northern Atlantic, my peace of mind was not further disturbed.

This first day was indeed a miserable initiation into the hitherto unknown horrors of the sea, and no greater contrast could be possible than the calm p. 17 of the night before and that wretched Sunday. It rained and blew great guns all day long, and by 6 p.m. the weather culminated in a severe gale, with the glass steadily falling, followed by a heavy thunderstorm, with vivid forked lightning. So furious indeed was the storm, that after passing Duncansby Head, and John o' Groat's House, our captain turned back and ran his vessel into Sinclair Bay, riding at anchor there for the night, not being willing, in the face of such weather, to attempt the 'Pentland Firth.'

The bay was calm, and the gentle movement of the waves was like the rocking of an arm-chair after the shaking and rolling we had experienced. We all enjoyed our dinner in peace, whilst the warmth of the cabin was a pleasant change from the searching cold on deck, which, despite furs and rugs, had pierced us through and through. Before we retired for the night, two other vessels had likewise put into the bay for safety from the elements, and here we were compelled to remain for forty-two hours while the storm still raged outside. Captain Robertson was a sensible man; when we asked him why he had put into Sinclair Bay, he said he considered it wiser to 'lay-to' for a few hours, and make up the time afterwards, rather than push on through such a gale, burning coal, and only making a knot or two an hour, perhaps not even that, straining the ship with her screw continually out of the water, making every one miserable, and gaining nothing. To this we all p. 18 agreed, so in quiet waters we passed a comfortable night, and consequently all the passengers put in an appearance next morning at breakfast.

As dirty weather was still reported ahead, we also spent Monday (a Bank holiday) in the bay. Alongside of us lay a large steamer, which had tried the Pentland Firth in the morning, but after five unsuccessful hours had been obliged to put back. This steamer had shifted her cargo, and lay over on her side, in a way that looked to me alarming; we left her in the bay when we weighed anchor on Tuesday at mid-day.

On the previous night some fishing boats put out from Keiss for herring fishing, and one came so near to us that we were tempted to prepare some letters and telegrams, a sailor on board our vessel saying he would try and drop them into the boat, in a basket. We tied them, therefore, up in a bag, with the necessary money for delivery, and watched their fate with anxiety. 'Letters,' shouted our sailor, but the fishermen shook their heads, evidently thinking it too rough to approach nearer to the steamer. Again the word 'Letters' was repeated, when another fishing smack responded 'Ay, ay,' and tacked, and as she shot past us, on our lee side, the basket was dropped over, accompanied by a bottle of whisky and ten shillings (the two latter being a *douceur* for the fishermen themselves) wrapped up for safety in an old rag, and tied to the bottom of the basket. The smack to which we thus confided our post was going out p. 19 for the night, but the men said they would put into Keiss next morning, and promised to send the letters ashore, which we afterwards found they did, whilst the bottle of whisky proved so acceptable a gift, that finding us still in Sinclair Bay on Tuesday morning, the fishermen brought some fresh herrings for breakfast, which they threw on board as they passed, and which proved an acceptable addition to our breakfast table.

The crew of the smack were a fine-looking set of men, well made, with handsome, frank faces—six men and a boy; but all they got for their night's danger and toil was some three dozen herrings. Such is the uncertainty of the deep.

Our ship's passengers numbered fourteen, exclusive of ourselves, and while we remained in Sinclair Bay, we had a good chance of criticising them. All good fellows, no doubt, but mostly of the trading class, and not very attractive, physically or mentally. There were two women in the number, the wife and daughter of a clothier resident in Iceland; but among the entire party we did not find any one likely to add to the sociability of the voyage, so, English-like, we kept to ourselves as much as possible.

How inconsistently some people dress on board ship! Our two women fellow-passengers did not often appear on deck, but when they did venture, despite the wind and rain, the elder wore an enormous hat, with a long, brown feather, which daily grew straighter, until all its curl had disappeared; p. 20 and a light-brown silk dress, on which every drop of rain or spray made its mark. She was a clothier's wife, and accustomed to sea-travelling; one would have imagined experience would have taught her the advisability of a less gorgeous style of apparel.

The girl wore a huge white sailor hat, covered with a profusion of red poppies, and her whole time seemed to be occupied in holding it on her head with both hands to prevent its blowing away. But it would rain, and the red from the poppies silently trickled all over the hat, and gradually formed rivulets on her face.

Then there was a very corpulent old man, with a large, square-patterned ulster, and a deer-stalker hat, tied on with a red silk handkerchief under his chin in a large bow, matching his complexion. His companion was thin and sallow, and wore a very desponding air, despite a prolific red beard, which, when we landed, caused much excitement among the Icelanders. I think their admiration made him feel shy, for after the demonstration made in its favour at the first landing port, he seldom went ashore, and even during the four days the *Camoens* lay off Reykjavik, he rarely left the ship.

Life on board ship is at the best monotonous, and we had to be contented with breathing the ozone, rejoicing in its health-giving properties, speculating as to the result of the voyage, and the novel scenes we hoped so soon to witness.

If ever cheap novels have their use, it is cer p. 21 tainly on board ship. Soaked with salt water or rain, it matters not; they most assuredly help to wile away many an hour, and even the usually non-novel reader is not ashamed to seize the telltale yellow-covered volume, and lose himself in its romance *pro tem*.

The second day we amused ourselves in making sketches of Noss Head, which one minute was enveloped in thick mist and rain, and the next stood out, clear and distinct, against a dull, grey sky.

When in the midst of our sketching, lo! quite an excitement prevailed among our ship's company, viz., the sight of a twenty-five feet bottle-nosed whale, which every one rushed to see, and which for some time played around the ship, accompanied by a couple of porpoise. The animal caused as much excitement as if it had been the mythical sea serpent itself. We saw them in dozens afterwards, but never with the same enthusiasm. Of course, the first whale had to be immortalised, and two of our party sketched and painted it; not without difficulty, however, for the rolling of the ship sent the water-colours or the turpentine sliding away at some critical moment of our work, and, on later occasions, chair, artist, picture, and colours were upset together in a disconsolate heap on the other side of the ship, much to every one's amusement.

Sketching at sea, in fact, is no easy matter, chiefly from the necessity of rapidity in the work; p. 22 while the smuts from the funnel are most exasperating, settling on the paper just where clear lights are most desirable, and—well, paint in oils on a rough day at sea, with a strong wind blowing the smoke towards you, and judge for yourself!

We left, as I said, our haven of refuge—Sinclair Bay—on Tuesday at noon, on a clear, bright day, but with a turbulent sea. However, we passed the Pentland Firth without having to run into the Orkneys for shelter, passing quite close to Pomona, round Duncansby Head and John o' Groat's House, a hideous modern hotel in the midst of a desolate bay.

Some people say that the story of John o' Groat's is merely mythical, and others declare he was a Scotchman, who, for ferrying folks across the Pentland Firth for fourpence, or a 'groat,' received his nickname. Again it is said that he was a Dutchman, with eight stalwart sons, who, having no idea of the law of primogeniture, alike wished to sit at the head of the table, whereupon John had an octagon table made, which, having neither top nor bottom, saved any wrangling for preeminence in his family.

Dunnet Head, which we next passed, is the most northerly point of Scotland. 'Stroma,' viz., the Orkneys, lay on our right, standing out in relief against a lovely sky—just such a picture as John Brett loves to paint.

We were all much struck by the variety of birds in the Pentlands—wild geese, ducks, northern p. 23 divers, and puffins, with, of course, the never absent gull. What a melancholy noise the gull makes, crying sometimes exactly like a child. And yet it is a pleasing companion on a desolate expanse of water, and most amusing to watch as it dives for biscuit or anything eatable thrown to it from the ship's side. Some of the gentlemen tried to capture them with a piece of fat bacon tied to a string; but although Mr Gull would swallow the bacon, he sternly refused to be landed.

p. 24

CHAPTER III.

LAND SIGHTED.

On leaving the choppy 'Pentland Firth,' we now entered on still rougher waters, encountering an Atlantic swell, caused by the previous storm. How the ship rolled! Walking on deck became impossible, while sitting in our deck chairs was nearly as bad, for they threatened to slide from under us. In despair we sought our berths, but to get into them in such a sea was a matter of difficulty, which practice in smooth waters had not taught us. Tuesday evening we bade adieu to the coast of Scotland, but what a boisterous night followed! Oh, dear! that eternal screw made sleeping at first impossible; we had not noticed its motion while on deck, but as soon as we laid our heads on our pillows, its monotonous noise seemed to grind our very brains. At last fatigue gained the victory, and I slept for some hours.

A sudden stoppage of the vessel awoke me at last with a start; it was still dark, but I heard loud talking and running about on deck overhead. Alarmed I sat up in my berth, and wondered what was the matter. All at once the screw p. 25 again revolved and then again stopped, and was once more in motion. We seemed to be going backward. I knew we were at least one hundred miles from Scotland, and there was no land nearer.

Wishing to learn what was going on, for in my half-awakened state, visions of icebergs and collisions rushed through my excited mind, I hastily summoned the stewardess, and asked what was the matter to cause such a commotion overhead. I learnt from her that an unusual and almost fatal event had just occurred. The man at the wheel, suddenly seized with a suicidal mania, had rushed from his post, possessed himself of two mops, which were lying on the deck, and putting one under each arm, with a wild and fiendish shriek had jumped overboard. The captain immediately stopped the ship and ordered a boat to be lowered; but owing to the high sea running, some time elapsed before this could be accomplished, and in the meantime the man had drifted some way from the vessel, and in the grey morning light his form was barely discernible in the trough of the waves. Notwithstanding the danger, the moment the boat was lowered there were no lack of volunteers to man her; but so persistent was the unfortunate man's resolve to perish, that he eluded all the efforts of his rescuers to capture him, and every time he was approached, swam away. The men at the oars had nearly given in, themselves soaked to the p. 26 skin, when a cheery call from the captain urged them on afresh.

It was only when exhaustion and numbness had rendered the poor maniac unconscious, that the sailors were able to pull him on board in an almost lifeless condition.

At breakfast time the captain informed us that the man's life had only been restored by constant rubbing; and that the poor creature seemed so violent, he had been obliged to have him locked up, probably a case of temporary insanity, which the captain attributed to the moon! For some days the poor deluded creature was very violent, and made many efforts to escape from his confinement. On one occasion he succeeded in getting half his body through a ventilating hole in his prison, from which he was extricated with great difficulty. The reason he assigned for jumping into the sea was that he feared being 'burnt alive,' in the boiler, a punishment in his aberration he fancied the captain had ordered for him.

As may be supposed, the event caused much excitement on board, at the same time practically diminishing our crew by two, as one man had constantly to be told off to look after the madman. His subsequent career was watched with great interest by those on board. His madness continued during the whole of the voyage, although sometimes he enjoyed lucid intervals, during which his chief desire was to sing, and he was permitted up on deck, when he amused himself by singing p. 27 sailor ditties and dancing hornpipes to his heart's content.

At other times his madness assumed a more dangerous form, and he had to be closely watched, to prevent him taking his own life. Every kindness was shown him by the captain and ship's officers and my brother attended him daily. When we reached Leith he was handed over to his relatives, and was subsequently put into an asylum, where I fear there was little chance of recovery, as madness was hereditary in his family.

As we steamed on, our voyage became somewhat monotonous, and we longed for the time to pass when we should reach the first trading port in Iceland, hoping there to imbibe new food for thought and comment. Our table was very fair; but a small steamer in a rough sea has many disadvantages in tempting the appetite. I must say the captain did all he could to make us comfortable, but he was not accustomed to carry lady passengers, and as the 'novelty of discomfort' began to wear off, it rendered us somewhat sensible to its unaccustomed yoke. There was a small smoking-room on deck, large enough to hold about eight persons, but which was always filled with smokers. The only other sitting-room was the saloon, the sofas of which were generally occupied by male passengers fast asleep, so we ladies had to choose between our berths and the deck, and we much preferred the latter in all weather, and under all circumstances. p. 28

Our fifth day at sea was one of utter misery. At dinner, despite the fiddles, the soup was landed in my lap, and a glass of champagne turned over before I had time to get it to my lips. I struggled through the meal bravely, and then went up on deck, but found it far too rough to walk about, while sitting down was only accomplished by holding fast to some friendly ropes tied near us with that view. About nine o'clock I sought my berth, but sleep was impossible, as most of my time was spent in trying to keep within the bounds of my bed, expecting that every successive lurch would eject me; whilst the port-holes having to be closed (that greatest of all discomforts in a storm) made the cabin close and unbearable.

The next morning, everybody had the same night's experience to relate, whilst the state of disorder our cabins were in, proved that we had not exaggerated our misery.

After leaving the Faroes on our right, we never sighted land for two days, nor did we even see a single ship; the one break in the monotony being the spouting of whales.

Two more days of terrible rolling amid those wild Atlantic breakers, which, as they washed our decks, seemed to sway the ship to and fro. Happily the wind was with us during the greater part of our voyage, and the captain crowded on all sail, making about 10 knots an hour.

Our first view of Iceland. *Etched by F. P. Fellows, from a sketch by the Author*, 1888.

On the Thursday following, we sighted Ice p. 29 land, and our spirits rose in proportion as we felt our voyage was nearing its completion. The sea, too, became calmer, and as we neared the coast the view was truly grand. At 10.30 p.m. the sun had not yet set, but was shedding its glorious evening glow over mountains which rose almost perpendicularly from the sea, and whose snow-clad peaks caught the rosy hues and golden tints of departing day. It was one of the most beautiful atmospheric effects I have ever witnessed, doubtless enhanced by the marvellous clearness of the atmosphere. I knew that Iceland was mountainous in its interior, but I had no idea that it had such a magnificent coast line, or such towering snow-capped hills. One thing we made special note of, namely, that while in the day time the thermometer rarely stood above 42°—10 above freezing point—it was very considerably lower at night, whilst instead of the damp cold we experienced during the day, at night the air was dry and frosty; the wind blowing from the north-west, and straight over the ice of Greenland, accounted for its being so sharp and keen.

It was well we had provided ourselves with furs and wraps of every possible warmth, for now indeed we required them all. Happily we only saw field ice in the distance, for had we come into nearer proximity with it, we should not have been able to pass round the north at all. No ice actually forms round the coast line, but the sea ice drifts from Greenland, 100 miles distant, caus p. 30 ing the north of the Island to be impassable, except during two or three months in the year.

The mean temperature of the south of Iceland is 39° F., in the central district 36° F., while in the north it is rarely above freezing point. During the winter of '80 and '81, when we were having what we thought great cold in England, the thermometer in Iceland was standing at 25° below zero, and polar bears were enjoying their gambols on its northern shores, having drifted thither on the ice from Greenland.

Iceland lies between N. Lat. 63, 23, 30, and 66, 32; and W. Long. 13, 32, 14, and 24, 34, 14; is 280 miles in length, and 180 to 200 miles in breadth.

Steaming up the east coast of the Island we breakfasted the next morning in the Arctic Circle, and what a delight it was to be there, the next best thing to being at the North Pole itself, and far more comfortable! We were also now in calm water, so could give vent to our excitement without fear of consequences. We had indeed had a terrible time of it since we left Scotland: even the captain acknowledged that the voyage had been unusually rough.

All that day we continued our course along the north-eastern coast of Iceland, in constant admiration of the magnificent wild scenery which broke upon our view. Snow capped-mountains rose almost abruptly from the sea, down which flowed little glacial rivulets, which emptied themselves p. 31 into the briny deep below. Another clear lovely evening, in which the quaint rocky outlines of the hills were discernible, with valleys, torrents, and glorious fjords, the whole embracing a panorama of miles of grand serrated coast line, showing to the greatest advantage in the curious evening glow.

So calm and beautiful was the scene, that all our party agreed it was worth a few days' discomfort in order to revel in the beauty of this bold Icelandic approach. The water was perfectly green, and as clear as possible, revealing innumerable yellow jelly-fish disporting themselves. We did not, however, see any of the sharks which are so frequently met with in these waters.

Entering the 'Oe Fjord' on our way to Akureyri, a small town lying some thirty miles from its mouth, as the evening lights shed their rich varied hues on all around, it was difficult to believe we could really be, after only a week's absence from home, so far north as the Arctic Circle, the more so as the rich warm colouring of the landscape resembled rather some southern clime.

We anchored off Akureyri at about eleven p.m., still in broad daylight, and I could read the smallest print at that hour without any difficulty, so short is the twilight of an Arctic summer. Real night there is none. This latter fact is most convenient for travellers, for being benighted in their explorations is an impossibility. If, however, the p. 32 Icelanders enjoy this prolonged daylight during their brief summer, how painful must be the reverse during the long winter, when they have but a few hours of daylight.

We were told an amusing story of an enterprising merchant from Glasgow, who, wishing to impress the Icelanders with the advantage of the electric light to cheer their long winter's darkness, went to Reykjavik in his large steam yacht, sending forth a proclamation inviting the natives to come and behold this scientific wonder. It was August, and he had not taken into consideration the fact that during that month there is no night in the Island, consequently his display was totally ineffectual!

After breakfast, a boat came alongside our steamer to convey us to the town. Off we went in a high state of pardonable excitement. All past discomfort was forgotten; we were about to set our feet on that *terra incognita* to most Europeans, viz., 'Iceland,' whose high mountain masses, varying in altitude from 3000 to 6800 feet, are, for the greater part of the year, covered with snow.

AKUREYRI (SHOWING LARGEST TREES IN ICELAND).

But before we land, let me describe the boat; large, of course, or it would never be able to stand the rough waters of the fjords, which, we were told, were often so turbulent as to render any communication with ships at sea impossible. Both ends of the boat are made alike, resembling two bows; our boat had neither rudder p. 33 nor stern, and required three men to handle each oar, one facing the other two, and all three pulling simultaneously. Sometimes the men stood up, their combined strength being thus apparently more effective in pulling through the rough sea which surrounded the Island. The oars were very thick at the rowlock, tapering off to an almost straight blade, not more than five inches wide. The men pulled well, and soon landed us amid the curious gaze of the inhabitants of the town, who had crowded down to the beach as soon as our steamer came in sight.

The first thing that struck us on landing was the sad, dejected look of the men and women who surrounded us. There was neither life nor interest depicted on their faces, nothing but stolid indifference. This apathy is no doubt caused by the hard lives these people live, the intense cold they have to endure, and the absence of variety in their every-day existence. What a contrast their faces afforded to the bright colouring and smiling looks one meets with in the sunny South.

The Icelanders enjoy but little sun, and we know ourselves, in its absence, how sombre existence becomes. Their complexions too, were very sallow, and their deportment struck us as sadly sober. A few of the women might possibly have been called pretty, notably two of their number, who possessed clear pale skins, good features, blue eyes, and lovely fair hair, which they wore braided in two long plaits, turned up, forming two loops p. 34 crossed on the crown of the head. These braids were surmounted by a quaint little black silk knitted cap, fitting close to the skull like an inverted saucer, and secured to the head by silver pins.

Hanging from this cap is a thick black silk tassel, from some six to ten inches long, which passes at the top through a silver tube, often of very pretty workmanship. I tried on one of these caps, and came to the conclusion that it was very becoming; thereon my vanity made me offer to purchase it, but as its owner asked twelve shillings, I declined to buy it, and afterwards procured one for half the sum in Reykjavik.

The bodices of the women's costumes are pretty, bound round two inches deep with black velvet, joined at the neck and waist with silver buckles; the bust is left open, showing a white linen shirt, sometimes ornamented with the finest embroidery; the skirt is short and full, and made of dark cloth.

A Native Woman. *Page 34*.
The men were of low stature, and

broadly built, and wore fur caps and vests, with huge mufflers round their throats. These latter, we observed, were mostly of a saffron colour, which, combined with their fur caps, tawny beards, and long locks, gave them a very quaint appearance. Men, women, and children alike wore skin shoes, made from the skin of the sheep or seal, cut out and sewn together to the shape of the foot, and pointed at the toe. These shoes are tied to their feet by a string made p. 35 of gut, and lined merely with a piece of flannel or serge, a most extraordinary covering in a country so rocky as Iceland, where at every step sharp stones, or fragments of lava, are encountered. Mocassins are also sometimes worn. The Icelanders, however, do not seem to mind any obstacles, but run and leap on or over them in their 'skin skurs' as though impervious to feeling. Later on we saw a higher class of Icelanders wearing fishermen's boots, but such luxuries were unknown in the little town where we first landed. The men being short of stature, in their curious kit much resembled Esquimaux.

The double-thumbed gloves worn were likewise a curiosity to us. These gloves have no fingers, but are made like a baby's glove, with a thumb at each side; and when rowing or at other hard work if the man wears out the palm of his glove, he simply reverses it and makes use of the other thumb. These gloves are generally knitted of grey wool, the thumbs being white, and resemble at a distance a rabbit's head with long ears. An Icelander always wears gloves, whether rowing, riding, fishing, washing, or sewing.

In ascertaining the number of days in a month we English people are accustomed to repeat a rhyme: the Icelander has a different mode of calculation. He closes his fist, calls his first knuckle January, the depression before the next knuckle February, when he arrives at the end, beginning again; thus the months that fall upon the knuckles, p. 36 are those containing thirty-one days, a somewhat ingenious mode of assisting the memory.

In our short trip to the Island, except on our visits to the geysers, which occupied four days, we invariably slept and dined on board the *Camoens*, making use of the time the steamer remained in each port to lionise the little towns we touched at, and to make such excursions into the interior as time permitted. In fact, except in the capital, there is not a really good hotel to be met with, although primitive accommodation may be found in the peasant dwellings and small hostelries.

THE FERRY BOAT.
p. 37

CHAPTER IV.

AKUREYRI.

Certainly the most noticeable feature, after a brief survey of the inhabitants of the place—at least such of them as surrounded us on landing—was the number of ponies massed together on the beach,—fine, sturdy, little animals, from eleven to thirteen hands high, stoutly made, with good hind quarters, thick necks, well-shaped heads, and tremendously bushy manes. Their feet and fetlocks are particularly good, or they could not stand the journeys. There were black, white, brown, chesnut, or piebald, but we did not see a single roan amongst them; a very quaint group they made standing quietly there, laden with every conceivable kind of saddle or pack. Many of the smaller ones were almost hidden by the size of the sacks, filled with goods, which were strapped on their backs. The pack ponies are never groomed, and badly fed, while the best riding ones are well stabled and looked after.

The scene that followed was interesting, for it appeared all these intelligent little animals were in attendance on their owners, men and women p. 38 alike, who had come down to the ship in order to barter the goods they had brought from the interior of the Island for flour, coffee, etc., on which they depend for their winter supplies. For hours these patient little ponies stood there, many of them with foals at their side, which latter, we were told, often get so footsore in their journeys as to require strapping upon their mothers' backs. The Icelanders are splendid riders, and are accustomed to the saddle from babyhood, for the roads are very bad, and the distances too great for walking, and there are no vehicles of any kind in Iceland. Some one indeed reported that one had been introduced into Reykjavik; we did not see it, but after once experiencing the nature of the roads, one can understand the absence of any wheeled conveyance. No ordinary springs could possibly stand the boulders of rock and lava, or the 'frost mounds,' over which the hardy Icelandic pony is accustomed to make his way. The native women ride man-fashion, a mode—as I shall later narrate—we ladies were compelled to adopt. For short distances a chair saddle is frequently used, somewhat resembling the writing-chair of an English study. The occupant sits sideways, having a board under her feet, in this way securing rest for the back. The ponies are intelligent and sure-footed, and require little or no guiding; but the amount of jogging and shaking which the rider is forced to undergo is tremendous—one wonders p. 39 they have any senses left. We had been fortunate in securing an introduction to Mr Stephenson, one of the chief officials of the Island, and also a native of the place, under whose escort we at once lionised the little town (if such it may be called), the second largest in Iceland. It consists of a collection of two-storied wooden houses, raised on a platform of lava blocks, plain and severe in structure, and painted yellow or white. Pretty muslin curtains and flowers adorn the windows, and as in this northern clime the keeping of flowers is no easy matter, the cultivation of them strikes one as highly praiseworthy. Inside the houses we found nicely polished floors, and simply furnished rooms, of a truly German style, stove included. The poorer abodes were mere hovels made of peat, admitting neither light nor air, and having the roofs covered with grass. One would have thought them almost uninhabitable, and yet I had seen dwellings nearly as bad around Killarney, and Glengariff.

What a hard life is that of the poor Icelanders! When our ship arrived, they were on the verge of starvation, their supplies being all exhausted. Glad indeed they must have been to welcome the *Camoens*, and know that flour and other staple articles of food were once again within their reach. Outside every house we noticed rows of dried fish hung up, and ready for the winter's consumption. Fish, but especially cod, is the staple food of the Icelander; but among the p. 40 poorest class this reserve consists more of fishes' heads, than fish *in toto*. What would a London epicure think of being obliged to feed for months together upon the heads of dried cod, which had for some weeks been exposed to the elements to render them hard and fit for eating. These heads are the refuse of fish, which are dried and exported to France, Spain, and England, and the heads not being required in these countries, are used by the Icelanders as food, being boiled down into a species of cake, which is eaten alike by the natives and their cattle, the liquid being given to the ponies.

Mr Stephenson told us that a large proportion of ponies thus fed died during the winter for lack of better nutriment.

A good riding pony in Iceland cost from £4 to £8, and a pack pony less: we hired them at 2s. 6d. a day. The breeding of these ponies is one of the great sources of livelihood, as the export last year numbered 3476. In the last voyage made by the *Camoens*, she brought home 975 of these hardy little animals, which gives some idea of the extent of the trade.

The smell of the fish while drying is terrible, the whole atmosphere being permeated with the odour. The streets are also paved with old fish heads and fish bones; indeed, at each port we touched, the smell of fish, fresh or dried, assailed eyes and noses in every direction. The population of Akureyri is under 1000, and is the residence of the Lieutenant p. 41 -Governor of the northern part of the Island. We visited one or two of the streets, hoping to meet with some curiosities, but pots, pans, kettles, and other domestic utensils of the most ordinary kind, alone met our view. In the eatable line, coarse brown sugar-candy seemed to abound, which the purchasers shovelled into bags or sacks, and carried off in quantities. We learnt that it is used by the Icelanders for sweetening coffee, having the double advantage of being pure sugar, and a hard substance resisting the damp which the snow engenders.

While in Akureyri we saw some poultry, perhaps half a dozen cocks and hens, but they were the only ones we met with in the Island; nor did we ever come across a pig! Fancy a land without these common accessories to a peasant's board! Eggs are only eaten on state occasions, and are considered a luxury, being imported from France; the eggs of the eider duck are considered very good food: they are, of course, only procurable round the coast.

Lord Dufferin gaily tells us, in his 'Letters from High Latitudes,' of an indiscriminating cock which was shipped at Stornway, and had become quite bewildered on the subject of that meteorological phenomenon 'the Dawn of Day.' It was questioned, in fact, whether he ever slept for more than five minutes at a stretch without waking up in a state of nervous agitation lest it should be cock crow, and at last, when night ceased altogether, his con p. 42 stitution could no longer stand the shock. Crowing once or twice sarcastically he went melancholy mad, and finally taking a calenture he cackled loudly (possibly of green fields), and then leapt overboard and drowned himself.'

Akureyri is both famous for, and proud of, its trees. There are actually five of them: these are almost the only trees in the Island. Miserable specimens indeed they appeared to us southerners, not being more than 10 feet high at most, and yet they were thought more of by the natives, than the chesnuts of Bushey Park by a Londoner.

The absence of wood in the Island is to a great extent overcome by the inhabitants collecting their fuel from the Gulf Stream, which brings drift wood in large quantities from Mexico, Virginia, the Caroline Islands, and even from the Pacific Ocean.

There is no lack of peat in certain districts, which, as in Ireland, is cut into square blocks, then stacked on to the ponies' backs till no pony is discernible, and thus conveyed to the farm, where it is used as fuel.

Indeed many of the houses are built of peat in the interior of the country where wood is not procurable. The peat for this purpose is cut in big blocks, thoroughly dried in the sun, and then it is easily cemented together with mud, thus making warm rooms, sheds, or passages to the farm houses.

Beautiful as much of the scenery was through which we passed, I must own that want of p. 43 foliage struck me as a terrible drawback to the perfection of the landscape, which, in other respects, was very wild and grand.

We dined at Akureyri at the little inn, which boasted of a fair-sized sitting-room, but not enough chairs to accommodate our party; so three sat in a row on an old-fashioned horsehair sofa, while we two ladies and our guest, Mr Stephenson, occupied the chairs. Our dinner consisted of soup, or rather porridge, of tapioca, flavoured with vanilla, a curiosity not known in Paris, I fancy; then a species of baked pudding, followed by some kind of a joint of mutton—but I am quite unable to say from what part of the sheep that joint was cut; no vegetables; black bread, and a kind of tea cake; bottled beer and corn brandy, augmented by coffee.

During our repast, Mr Stephenson gave us much information about the Island. He told us a bank had lately been opened in the capital, which he hoped would soon be followed by a branch at Akureyri, a progress of civilisation which must of necessity circulate money more freely, and make the present system of barter less common—ponies, sheep, fish, etc., being now given in preference to money in exchange for goods.

Sending or receiving money in Iceland anywhere except in its capital, is a difficult matter, as there is no organised post office method for such transactions.

The following history and constitution of the p. 44 bank in Reykjavik, furnished me by Mr Gordon, may be interesting to my readers.

'There is one bank, the State Bank. Its capital consists of the revenues of the Island; there are no shareholders. The manager is an Icelander, who has one assistant only, who keeps the books. Two inspectors or auditors are appointed by the Governor of Iceland. The Bank has just been started under the control of the Governor and Council of Iceland; and on the 1st July 1886 began an issue of State notes—legal tender in Iceland only. Danish notes are also tender in Iceland, though the reverse is not the case. The issue is limited to Kr. 500,000, or £27,777. They are issued against the security of the revenues of the Island, and they are forced on the people, who do not as yet take to them, and no wonder, considering the great want of communication even in the summer months. They are convertible for either silver or gold at Reykjavik. Branch banks will probably be opened at Akureyri, Seydisfjord, and Isafjord. The Bank publishes a statement of its affairs periodically. The Bank charges 6 per cent., as a rule, on advances, and grants 3 per cent. on deposits. The Bank advances against land, and houses (the latter in the capital only, as they cannot be insured elsewhere against fire), and personal security. The advances are said to stand at Kr. 130,000, or £7222. When against personal security a promissory note is taken, signed by the borrower and two irresponsible witnesses, or by p. 45 two responsible obligants, according to standing. Title-deeds are taken as collateral security. The Bank has its own forms for loan-documents. The probability is that the Bank will soon become the possessor of a great deal of property in houses and land in Iceland, as bad seasons are frequent, which prevent prompt payment.'

ICELANDIC AND ENGLISH MONEY TABLE.

		£	s.	d.			
7½	öre,	0	0	1	Kr.	9.00	öre
15	"	0	0	2	"	9.90	"
22½	"	0	0	3	"	10.80	"
30	"	0	0	4	"	11.70	"
37½	"	0	0	5	"	12.60	"
45	"	0	0	6	"	13.59	"
52½	"	0	0	7	"	14.40	"
60	"	0	0	8	"	15.30	"
67½	"	0	0	9	"	16.20	"
75	"	0	0	10	"	17.10	"
82½	"	0	0	11	"	18.00	"
90	"	0	1	0	"	36.00	"
Kr. 1.80	"	0	2	0	"	54.00	"
" 2.70	"	0	3	0	"	72.00	"
" 3.60	"	0	4	0	"	90.00	"

"	4.50	"	0	5	0	"	108.00	"
"	5.40	"	0	6	0	"	126.00	"
"	6.30	"	0	7	0	"	144.00	"
"	7.20	"	0	8	0	"	162.00	"
"	8.10	"	0	9	0	"	180.00	"

After dinner, we visited the small Lutheran Church. Unfortunately we had no opportunity of attending a service, though, to judge from the plainness of the ecclesiastical buildings, such p. 46 must be very simple. The clergyman wears a black gown, and an enormous white Elizabethan frill, with a tight-fitting black cap. This little church accommodates about 100 persons, and in place of pews, has merely wooden forms. Over the altar was an old painting of the crucifixion, done by a native artist, and surrounded by a little rail. The walls were plainly whitewashed, the windows bare, and no musical instrument was visible. There was, however, both a font and a pulpit.

The town boasts of a hospital, a free library, and two printing establishments. At night we returned to our ship quarters.

The next day, there being nothing more to be seen in Akureyri, we decided to take a ride, in order to visit a waterfall, which Mr Stephenson told us would repay the fatigue, and also give us some idea of what an Icelandic expedition was like. Truly that first ride is a never-to-be-forgotten experience. Our road lay over rough stones, and 'frost-mounds.' These latter are a recognised feature in Icelandic travel; they are small earth hillocks, about 2½ feet wide and 2 feet high, caused, according to Professor Geikie, by the action of the frost. In some parts these mounds cover the ground, lying close to each other, so as to leave little or no room for the ponies to step between, and they have to walk over them, a movement which sways the rider from side to side, causing many a tumble even p. 47 to experienced native horsemen. It is like riding over a country graveyard,

'Where heaves the turf in many a mouldering heap.'

As to road, there was none, nor is there such a thing in Iceland worthy of the name. The rider merely turns his pony's head in the direction he wishes to go, and it picks its own way far better than he could guide it. The bridle used is a curious workmanship of knotted rope or thick string with a brass curb or bit, ornamented by some queer head or device. The saddles are equally quaint. Those of the women I have already described; those of the men are made very high, both in front and behind, somewhat like a Mexican saddle, there being a hollow in the centre. A crupper is always used, and straps are attached to the back of the saddle, from which the farmer hangs his sealskin bags, containing an *omnium gatherum* of his lighter goods.

The ponies are very slightly girthed, nor, indeed, would it do to tighten them, so old and rotten is the usual paraphernalia for their equipment that an attempt in this direction would bring the whole thing to grief, which species of *contretemps* we met with more than once during our rides. In fact, a small English side-saddle and bridle would be not only a most useful addition to a lady's luggage, but add much to her safety and comfort.

While at Akureyri, Mr Stephenson kindly lent p. 48 us two ladies' saddles, or we should never have accomplished that first ride. They were old-fashioned two-pommeled ones, with gorgeously-embroidered cushions, on which we were supposed to sit, and marvellous saddle-cloths; and we realised we were travellers in earnest when once we mounted and started. Icelandic ponies walk well, and are also trained to pace, a movement closely resembling that of an American runner. This is a motion which requires experience, as it is too quick to rise without practice, and too rough to sit still in the saddle. Some of the ponies trotted, others cantered well, but one had to make them understand one wanted them to do so, as the usual Icelandic mode of riding is that of 'pacing,' at which the animals continue for hours. Later in our trip, when we visited the Geysers, we had to ride over 40 miles a day, in order to cover the distance in time to catch our steamer on its return voyage, and thus became well acquainted with pony riding in all its various modes of procedure.

It did not take us long to reach the Gléra waterfall, which was very pretty, about a mile from the fjord, and formed by the river: trout can sometimes be caught in the pool beneath the fosse.

Perhaps the most noticeable feature of Akureyri was the shark oil manufactory between that little town and Oddeyri, the stench of which was something so fearful that I know of nothing that could possibly compare with it. In certain winds it can be smelt for miles. The manufacture of cod liver p. 49 oil is bad enough, but that of shark oil is even worse. Luckily, the establishments where such oil is made are not numerous, and are principally confined to such out-of-the-way regions as Iceland and Greenland.

At Oddeyri there was another store of great importance to the natives, viz., a large meat preserving place, where great preparations were in active progress for the coming winter.

Not far distant from here lives a very remarkable man, a self-taught artist of considerable power, who has never been out of the Island, consequently has but rarely seen a picture, and yet his artistic instincts and power of representation are of no mean order; and more especially displayed in his altar pieces. I wonder what he would say to those of Rubens or Vandyck! This man has the greatest love of animals, and was surrounded, when we visited him, by a number of dogs of the Icelandic breed, small animals closely resembling the Pomeranian, with long coats and sharp stand-up ears, which always give a knowing look to the canine head. Most of them seemed to be black, though not a few were a rich sable brown. They are pretty beasts. I don't believe there is a cat in the Island, leastways we never saw one, wild or tame, during our sojourn there. The domesticated cat, fowls, and pigs are practically unknown in these climes.

Some 20 miles from Akureyri once lived another interesting man, Sira Jon Thorlackson, a well p. 50 known native poet, many of whose verses are dear to his countrymen; in his lifetime he undertook and accomplished a translation of Milton's 'Paradise Lost'

There are some 20,000 specimens of butterflies scattered over the world, and yet in Iceland these species are unknown, although insects of certain kinds do exist, especially mosquitos, as we learnt to our cost. Although there are no butterflies, and but few insects, flowers abound.

An Agricultural College has lately been established in the vicinity of Akureyri, the headmaster having formerly been one of the librarians of the Advocates' Library in Edinburgh. No doubt the natives will learn to drain their bogs and swamps, level their frost mounds, and produce more out of the earth than at present, with the help of this much needed institution.

How terribly soon that curse of modern civilisation, drunkenness, spreads! It was Sunday when we first landed at Akureyri, and I am sorry to say not a few of its inhabitants had imbibed more corn brandy than was good for them; it seemed to have the effect of making them maudlingly affectionate, or else anxious to wrestle with everybody.

The two days the *Camoens* lay off Akureyri gave us no time for prolonged excursions, but was more than sufficient to lionise the little town, so we were not sorry when the steamer's whistle summoned us to return to our floating home.

Ten hours' further journey and our anchor was p. 51 dropped opposite Sauderkrok, an even smaller town than Akureyri, with its 1000 inhabitants, but which interested us more from its very primitive population, If the reader will follow the steamer's course in the map, he will find Sauderkrok marked in its direct course.

p. 52

CHAPTER V.

HISTORICAL NOTES.

Before proceeding to narrate more of our own experiences of Iceland, I have ventured to collate the following memoranda of the early history of the Island, from Mr George Lock's, F.R.G.S., 'Guide to Iceland,' a most valuable appendage to a traveller's luggage in that Island; the few notes gathered from its pages and other guidebooks will enable my readers to follow my narrative with greater interest; whilst I trust this open acknowledgment of my piracy will be forgiven.

It has been ascertained that before the year 874 Iceland was almost an uninhabited Island, being occupied only by a few natives, Culdee Monks, who having seceded from the Roman Catholic faith, retired there for safety and quiet.

Prior to its settlement it was circumnavigated by a Swede, who landed, it is said, and wintered there, and in 868, Flóki Vilgertharsson, a mighty Viking, visited it, who gave it the present name of Iceland.

The first permanent settlers were of the Norse race; two men who, banished from their country, p. 53 fitted out a ship and sailed to Iceland, where in 874 they made a settlement in the south of the island.

Later Harold Haarfager, a tyrannical and warlike spirit, who was fast extending his kingdom over Norway, so offended many of his subjects, among them several powerful chiefs, that the latter, to avoid further warfare, quitted the land of their birth, and went to settle in Iceland.

This emigration in due time peopled it, until sixty years later its population was calculated at 50,000, which has now increased to 72,000. Most of the settlers came from Norway, supplemented by a few from the Orkneys, Scotland, and Ireland. One of the fjords bears the name of 'Patrick's Fjord,' after an Irish Bishop.

The climate of Iceland at this early date seems to have been a far more moderate one than at the present time, a fact established by scientific research.

In the early days of the Island, the Norse chiefs who took possession of it appropriated to themselves large tracts of country, distributing them among their own retainers; these latter in return swore allegiance to their separate chiefs, undertaking to support them in their private quarrels, whilst they were themselves in this manner protected from aggression.

Every Norse chieftain of any note established a 'Hof' or Temple in his own lands, whilst the yearly sacrificial feasts were supported by a tax gathered from the people. Each chief reigned p. 54 supreme within his own jurisdiction, and could take life or confiscate property at will. At given periods these feudal rulers met to discuss affairs of importance, or to promulgate laws for the better government of the community; but they had no written laws, or any general accepted body of lawgivers, hence, as may easily be supposed, constant differences of opinion existed, which per force was settled by an appeal to arms. Such a state of things, where 'might became right,' could not continue long amid such a warlike nation as the Norsemen, and in 926 the principal chiefs of the Island took steps to form a Commonwealth, and established a code of laws for its government. It was for some time a question where this primitive national assembly should meet, and finally a rocky enclosure, situated in a sunken plain, cut off by deep rifts from the surrounding country, was selected. This spot, so romantic in position, so safe from intrusion, so associated with the early government of the Island, was called 'Thingfield,' or 'speaking place'—Thingvaller it is now termed—and here the first Althing was held in 929; at the same period 'Logmen' or law-givers were appointed, to whom universal reference on legal questions was referred.

This 'Althing' combined both the power of a High Parliament and that of a Court of Justice, and before the introduction of Christianity into the Island, its members were called upon to swear upon a sacred ring, brought for the purpose from the p. 55 temple of the High Priest, to administer both 'with justice and clemency.'

About the time William of Normandy invaded England, Godred Crovan, son of Harold the Black of Iceland, conquered the Isle of Man, in whose family it remained for some centuries. Probably through this Norse connection the custom of proclaiming the laws to the people in this latter Isle from a hill in the open air was first introduced, although now discarded by the Althing in Iceland and in various Northern Isles. In the Isle of Man the laws are still read to the people on 5th July on Tynwald Hill; of late years they have only been read in English, but until 1865 they were also proclaimed in the Manx language (which is nearly related to Gaelic); many of the natives not speaking or even understanding English.

According to Joseph Train's 'Historical Notes on the Isle of Man,' 'the great annual assembly of the Islanders at the Tynwald Hill, on the Feast day of St John the Baptist, is thus described in the Statute Book,—"Our doughtful and gracious Lord, this is the Constitution of old time, the which we have given in our days: First, you shall come thither in your Royal Array, as a King ought to do, by the Prerogatives and Royalties of the Land of Mann; and upon the Hill of Tynwald sitt in a chaire, covered with the royall cloath and cushions, and your visage unto the east, and your sword before you, holden with the point upwards; your barrons in the third degree sitting beside you, and p. 56 your beneficed men and your Deemsters before you sitting; and your Clarkes Knights, Esquires, and Yeomen, and yeoman about you in the third degree; and the worthiest man in your Land (these are the twenty-four Keys) to be called in before your Deemsters, if you will ask any Thing of them, and to hear the Government of your Land and your will; and the Commons to stand without the circle of the Hill with three Clarkes in their surplisses."'

Even at the present day this ceremony continues in the Isle of Man, as above said. When the officials arrive at the Tynwald Hill, the Governor and Bishops take their seats, surrounded by the Council and the Keys, the people being assembled on the outside to listen.

From the establishment of the Althing until the 11th century, the Icelanders seem to have managed their internal affairs with moderation and discretion; at least little of importance connected with the Island is recorded until the discovery of Greenland by Eric the Red, which subsequently led to that of America, towards the end of the 10th century, by Biono Herioljorm, and before the time of Columbus.

CHRONOLOGICAL DATES.
Colonised, 874.
First Althing sat, 929.
Christianity introduced, 1000.
Snorri Sturlusson murdered, 1241, 22d Sept.
Had a republic and a flourishing literature, till subjected to Hakon, King of Norway, 1264.
Iceland fell under Danish rule, 1380. p. 57
Protestantism (Lutheranism) introduced about 1551.
Famine through failure of crops, 1753-54.
Greatest volcanic eruptions, 1783.
New Constitution signed by the King Christian of Denmark on his visit to Iceland when the 1000th anniversary of the colonisation of Iceland was celebrated, 1874, 1 Aug.
Eruption of 1783 destroyed 10,000 men.
" " 28,000 ponies.
" " 11,500 cows.
" " 200,000 sheep.
Latest great eruption 1875.
The following curious custom is copied from Dr Kneeland's book:—

'In their pagan age, it was the custom for the father to determine, as soon as a child was born, whether it should be exposed to death or brought up; and this not because the rearing of a deformed or weak child would deteriorate a race which prided itself on strength and courage, but from the inability of the parents, from poverty, to bring up their offspring. The newly born child was laid on the ground, and there remained untouched until its fate was decided by the father or nearest male relative; if it was to live, it was taken up and carried to the father, who, by placing it in his arms, or covering it with his cloak, made himself publicly responsible for its maintenance. It was then sprinkled with water, and named. This was regarded in pagan times as sacred as the rite of baptism by Christians, and after its performance it was murder to expose it. The usual mode of desertion was either to place the infant in a covered p. 58 grave, and there leave it to die, or to expose it in some lonely spot, where wild animals would not be likely to find it. After the introduction of Christianity, such exposure was permitted only in cases of extreme deformity.'

In 997, the first Christian missionary, Thangbrand, landed in Iceland, and preached Christianity to its inhabitants by fire and sword; but the severity with which he tried to enforce his views, failed to convince the people to give up Paganism. Two years later, however, Iceland threw off the heathen yoke, and embraced the Roman Catholic religion. Early in the 11th century, several Icelanders visited Europe to study in its various universities, whilst churches and schools were established in the Island, taught by native bishops and teachers, and with such marvellous rapidity did education spread among the people, that it reached its culminating point in the 13th century, when the literary productions of the Icelanders became renowned through Europe during what was termed the Dark Ages.

'Iceland shone with glorious lore renowned,
A northern light when all was gloom around.
Montgomery.

Towards the end of the 12th century the peace of Iceland was broken up by internal struggles for power, which resulted in the loss of its independence. So wide-spread, in fact, had become these internal feuds, that at last some of the chiefs, refusing to submit to have their differences settled p. 59 by the laws of the country, visited Norway, and solicited the help of its king, Hakon the Old.

Now this king had long been ambitious to annex Iceland to his dominions, and in lieu of settling the disputes brought before him, by an amicable arrangement between the Icelandic chiefs, he only fomented their quarrels, and finally persuaded a number of them to place Iceland under his sceptre. This they agreed to do, and, after much bloodshed, in 1264 Iceland was annexed to Norway, and its far-famed little republic became extinct.

The history of the Island since that date has been a mournful one. Until thirty years since, the conquest of their Island by Norway, left in its train nothing but apathy and discontent among its inhabitants; in fact, the poor Icelanders, when once they realised their loss of independence, seemed to have neither spirit nor power to rise above the state of suicidal slavery into which they had fallen through their political differences.

In 1848, however, an heroic band of patriots combined, and fought bravely to rescue their country from the degrading condition into which it had fallen; but its long subjection to a foreign yoke has left, it is feared, a lasting impression on the character of its inhabitants, and this, combined with their great poverty, has engendered a sadness and soberness of spirit which they seem unable to overcome.

In 1830, Norway was united to Denmark, and p. 60 Iceland was transferred to the Danish crown. In 1851 the Icelanders threw off the Roman Catholic supremacy, and embraced the Lutheran form of worship.

In 1800 their time-honoured institution, viz., 'The Althing,' was done away with, and for the subsequent forty-three years Danish rule prevailed. In 1843, however, the former state of government was re-established, but only in a very limited form, the power granted to it being but a shadow of its former self, whilst its sittings were removed from the rocky fortress where it had so long held sway, to the capital, Reykjavik, a large stone building having been erected for its deliberations.

In 1848, when Denmark proclaimed its Constitution, the Icelanders in a body petitioned that the full power of the Althing should be restored. For many years this petition was presented in vain, until King Christian visited the Island, signed a new and separate Constitution for Iceland in January 1873, at the same time retaining certain prerogatives.

In size Iceland is somewhat larger than Ireland, its area being calculated at 38,000 square miles. Geographically it lies south of the south of the Arctic Circle, about 650 miles north-west of Duncansby Head. Its eastern, northern, and north-western coasts are deeply indented with a number of narrow fjords, whilst the southern coast, on the contrary, has not a bay or fjord capable of affording a harbour to even a small vessel.

A group of islands, called Westmannaggar, or p. 61 Irishmen's Isles, lie off the south coast, and in the various bays on its western coast are innumerable smaller islets.

The interior of the Island is mostly a broad barren plateau, from which rise ice-clad mountains and sleeping volcanoes. Its inhabited regions lie along the coast, where there are small tracts which repay cultivation. The area of the lava deserts, viz., tracts of country covered with lava which has flowed down from volcanic mountains, is computed at 2400 square miles, whilst there are 5000 square miles of vast stony uncultivated wastes—nearly one seventh of the entire area—which apparently increase in extent.

The Island consists of 'Toklar,' or glaciers, and coned heights known as 'Vatna Toklar,' 'Läng Tökull,' 'Dranga,' and 'Glamu Toklar,' and a group of mountains called 'Töklar Guny' in the south of the Island.

The area of pasture land all over Iceland is estimated at 15,000 English miles, but a large part of this is moorland, whilst, sad to say, the pasture land is visibly diminishing, and the sandy wastes increasing. This, to a certain extent, is due to the want of industry of the natives.

In 1875 no less than 1000 square miles was buried beneath an eruption of pumice, but it is considered that the action of the frost and rain upon this porous substance will eventually fertilise the soil and permit of its cultivation. Iceland is the most volcanic region of the earth. p. 62

The Island has four large lakes and innumerable small rivers, none of which are navigable beyond a short distance from the mouth. It is not possible to enter here at large on the volcanic features of the Island, but a short chapter has been appended at the end of the volume touching on the principal volcanoes, their action and eruptions.

PONIES FORDING A RIVER.
p. 63

CHAPTER VI.

SAUDERKROK—RIDING.

At a short distance from shore, Sauderkrok, appeared to us at first a most forlorn-looking little settlement, consisting of some few dozen wooden houses and peat hovels. However, on a closer acquaintance with the place, during the two days the steamer remained in port to enable our captain to unload some 200 tons of cargo, we found plenty of things to interest us in the little town.

There being no warehouses, or even sheds, to store the newly arrived goods, they were piled on the beach, and there sold by auction. It was a most amusing scene, the whole population turning out to witness, or take part in, the bidding for the goods thus sold.

The goods were piled up in a half circle, the auctioneer sitting on a table in the middle, assisted by one or two of the chief town's folk. Outside the circle stood men, women, and children from all surrounding parts of the Island; beyond them again, the patient little ponies waiting for the loads they were to carry off inland. Much of the sale was carried on by barter, a system of trading not wholly comprehensible to us strangers, p. 64 although we saw the natives offer specimens of what they had to exchange. As onlookers, such a novel exhibition afforded a fine field for the study of Icelandic physiognomy, the expressions of anxiety, pleasure, or disappointment being depicted on their faces when the coveted goods were knocked down to the would-be purchaser, or not. To these poor people this must have been a meeting of the greatest importance, as their winter comforts mostly depended thereon; but such is their habitual apathy, that even this great event caused little outward excitement.

No sooner were the goods purchased, than the ship's crew sorted them out, and with the help of an interpreter they were handed over to their owners, some of whom within a few hours were starting off on their homeward journey; a considerable part of the goods, however, still remained on the shore when we left two days later, the purchasers having arranged to return for future loads.

In 1883 the imports amounted to £337,000, from bread, groceries, wines, beer, spirits, tobacco, and stuffs. Trade has been open to all nations since 1854.

THE EXPORTS OF ICELAND IN 1887.

Salted cod	cwt.	112,201	value	£13
Other salted fish	"	57,226	"	46,8
Salted herring	barrels	27,096	"	20,0
Salted salmon	cwt.	218	"	763 65
Cod oil	barrels	1,215	"	2,73
Shark oil	"	7,508	"	22,5
Seal oil	"	121	"	336
Whale oil	"	230	"	460
Ponies	numbers	3,476	"	10,4
Sheep	"	10,000	"	10,0
Wool	cwt.	12,134	"	47,5
Salted mutton	"	9,336	"	11,9
Eider down	lbs.	7,149	"	5,41

besides woollen stockings and gloves, skins, feathers, tallow, dried fish, sounds, and roes.

Sauderkrok was to witness a new experiment in our mounting arrangements. On our arrival, as usual we intended riding into the interior, and applied at the only inn in the place for ponies, when to our discomfiture we learnt no such thing as a lady's side-saddle was to be obtained. The innkeeper and our party held a long consultation as to what was to be done, during which the inhabitants of the place gathered round us in full force, apparently much interested in our proceedings.

At last one of the lookers-on disappeared, and presently returned in triumph with a chair-saddle, such as already described, used by the native women. This was assigned to Miss T. No second one, however, was obtainable, and I had to choose between remaining behind or overcoming the difficulties of riding lady fashion on a man's saddle. My determination was quickly taken, and much to the amusement of our party, up I mounted, the whole village stolidly watching the proceeding, whilst the absence of pommel contributed considerably to the difficulty I had in keeping my seat. p. 66

Off we started, headed by our guide, and as long as the pony walked I felt very comfortable in my new position, so much so that I ventured to try a trot, when round went the saddle and off I slipped. Vaughan came to my rescue, and after readjusting the saddle, and tightening the girths, I remounted, but only with the same result. How was I to get along at this rate?

Our Mode of Riding. *Page 66*.

I had often read that it was the custom for women in South America, and in Albania, who have to accomplish long distances on horseback, to ride man fashion. Indeed, women rode so in England, until side-saddles were introduced by Anne of Bohemia, wife of Richard II., and many continued to ride across the saddle until even a later date. In Iceland I had seen women ride as men, and felt more convinced than ever that this mode was safer and less fatiguing. Although I had ridden all my life, the roughness of the Icelandic roads and ponies made ladywise on a man's saddle impossible, and the sharpness of the pony's back, riding with no saddle equally so. There was no alternative: I must either turn back, or mount as a man. Necessity gives courage in emergencies. I determined therefore to throw aside conventionality, and do in 'Iceland as the Icelanders do.' Keeping my brother at my side, and bidding the rest ride forward, I made him shorten the stirrups, and hold the saddle, and after sundry attempts succeeded in landing myself man fashion on the animal's back. The position felt p. 67 very odd at first, and I was also somewhat uncomfortable at my attitude, but on Vaughan's assuring me there was no cause for my uneasiness, and arranging my dress so that it fell in folds on either side, I decided to give the experiment a fair trial, and in a very short time got quite accustomed to the position, and trotted along merrily. Cantering was at first a little more difficult, but I persevered, and in a couple of hours was quite at home in my new position, and could trot, pace, or canter alike, without any fear of an upset. The amusement of our party when I overtook them, and boldly trotted past, was intense; but I felt so comfortable in my altered seat that their derisive and chaffing remarks failed to disturb me. Perhaps my boldness may rather surprise my readers; but after full experience, under most unfavourable circumstances, I venture to put on paper the result of my experiment.

Riding man-fashion is less tiring than on a side-saddle, and I soon found it far more agreeable, especially when traversing rough ground. My success soon inspired Miss T. to summon up courage and follow my lead. She had been nearly shaken to pieces in her chair pannier, besides having only obtained a one-sided view of the country through which she rode; and we both returned from a 25 mile ride without feeling tired, whilst from that day till we left the Island, we adopted no other mode of travelling. I am quite sure had we allowed conventional scruples to p. 68 interfere, we should never have accomplished in four days the 160 miles' ride to the Geysers, which was our ultimate achievement.

I may here mention our riding costume. We had procured very simply made thick blue serge dresses before leaving home, anticipating rough travelling. The skirts being full and loose, hung well down on either side when riding, like a habit on the off and near sides, and we flattered ourselves that, on the whole, we looked both picturesque and practical. Our very long waterproof boots (reaching above the knee) proved a great comfort when fording rivers, which in an Iceland ride are crossed every few miles, sometimes oftener. For the rest, we wore ordinary riding attire.

The crooked position of a side-saddle—for one must sit crooked to look straight—is very fatiguing to a weak back, and many women to whom the exercise would be of the greatest benefit, cannot stand the strain; so this healthy mode of exercise is debarred them, because Society says they must not ride like men. Society is a hard taskmaster. Nothing is easier than to stick on a side-saddle, of course, and nothing more difficult than to ride gracefully.

For comfort and safety, I say ride like a man. If you have not courage to do this, in visiting Iceland take your own side-saddle and bridle (for a pony), as, except in Reykjavik, horse furniture is of the most miserable description, and the constant breakages cause many p. 69 delays, while there are actually no side-saddles, except in the capital, and a chair is an instrument of torture only to be recommended to your worst enemy.

On one occasion, while the rest of the party were settling and arranging about ponies, which always occupied some time, I sat down to sketch on a barrel of dried fish, and was at once surrounded by men, women, and children, who stood still and stared, beckoning to all their passing friends to join them, till quite a crowd collected.

They seemed to think me a most extraordinary being. The bolder ones of the party ventured near and touched me, feeling my clothes, discussed the material, and calmly lifted my dress to examine my high riding-boots, a great curiosity to them, as they nearly all wear the peculiar skin shoes already described. The odour of fish not only from the barrel on which I was seated, but also from my admiring crowd, was somewhat appalling as they stood around, nodding and chatting to one another.

Their interest in my sketch was so great I cannot believe they had ever seen such a thing before, and I much regretted my inability to speak their language, so as to answer the many questions I was asked about it all. I fancied they were satisfied, however, for before going away, they one and all shook hands with me, till my hand quite ached from so many friendly grasps.

The men in Iceland always kiss one another p. 70 when they meet, as also do the women, but I only once saw a man kiss a woman!

'Snuffing' is a great institution. The snuff is kept in a long box, like a gourd, often a walrus tooth, with a long brass mouth. This they put right up the nostril, turning the head to do so—a very dirty and uncouth habit, but one constantly indulged in by both sexes. They also smoke a great deal. On one occasion Vaughan gave a guide some tobacco. He took it, filled his pipe, and put it back in his pocket, shaking his head as much as to say he could not light his pipe in the wind. This dilemma was overcome by Vaughan offering a fusee. The man took it, looked at it, and grinned. So Vaughan showed him how to use it, and struck a light. His astonishment and amusement were so overwhelming that he got off his pony, and rolled about on the ground with delight. He had evidently never seen such a curiosity before.

We rode to Reykir, 10 or 12 miles from Sauderkrok, where there are hot springs. The road was very bad, and it took us nearly three hours to accomplish the distance, but this may be partly accounted for by our stopping every half-hour to mend some one's broken harness. My only girth, a dilapidated old thing, was mended with string, and when trotting along soon after starting, the saddle and I both rolled off together, the only fall I have ever had in my life, and from a little Icelandic pony too! I was thoroughly disgusted p. 71 at the accident, and my want of balance. However, I soon had occasion to comfort myself on my easy fall, when our guide and pony turned three complete somersaults down a hill, the man disappearing. But he soon rolled out from beneath the animal, shook himself, and mounted once again. How every bone in his body was not broken I can't imagine, so rough and strewn with lava boulders, was the ground on which he fell.

Shortly after our party had left Sauderkrok, a young Icelander was noticed riding after us, and when my fall occurred, he advanced towards us politely, and offered me the use of his pony and saddle, which I gratefully accepted, and he mounted mine, riding without any girths, and gracefully balancing himself in a most marvellous manner. This new addition to our party proved a very valuable one, as he talked English perfectly, and was most intelligent and communicative. He told us he was on his way to Copenhagen to study languages, preparatory to trying for a professorship at Reykjavik, and we found he had already mastered English, French, Latin, and Danish. His name never transpired, but we learnt that as soon as the news reached him that an English party had landed and started for 'Reykir,' he had saddled a pony and ridden after us, wanting to see what we were like, and also to endeavour to make our acquaintance, and thus be able to air his English with English people, for until then he had never spoken it p. 72 except with his teacher. My fall gave him the opportunity he wanted, as he was then able to offer his services without intrusion, which he did with the politest manners.

The Icelanders are a wonderfully well-educated people. Our new friend told us he did not believe there was a man or woman in the Island who could not read and write, and certainly on our visits to the various farm-houses, we never failed to notice a Lutheran Bible, and many of the old 'Sagas,' by native poets, beside translations of such works as Shakespear, Goëthe, John Stuart Mill's 'Political Economy,' and other well-known writings.

Icelandic is the oldest of the present German dialects, being purer than the Norwegian of to-day, and its literature dates from 1057, immediately after the introduction of writing.

The literature has been ascertained to be of so deeply interesting a character, that the fact of establishing an 'Icelandic Chair' in one of our Universities is now, I believe, under consideration. Many of the natives speak, and understand, Danish—indeed the laws are read to them in that language; and between Danish and Icelandic, we ladies succeeded in making our German understood. Icelandic is now given with English and Anglo-Saxon as optional subjects for the examination at Cambridge for the Modern Language Tripos.

Appended are a few Icelandic sentences, which we found useful in our travels. They are spelt p. 73 phonetically, as we learnt a few phrases from such of the guides as could speak a little English.

G. C. Locke, in his most interesting work 'The Home of the Eddas,' in speaking of Icelandic literature, says, 'Might not some of the hours so fruitlessly spent in misinterpreting incomprehensible Horace be more fitly devoted to the classics of Northern Europe?. Snovri Sturluson the author of the "Elder Edda," has no compeer in Europe.'

Can you lend us any ponies?	Getithir launath okir hesta?
Can you give us five ponies?	Getithir launath okir fim hesta?
No; I cannot lend you so many.	Neg; jeg getiki launath īkur (īdhur when speaking to one person) sō mārga.
I can give you two.	Jeg gyet launath tvōa.
How many?	Kwādh mārga
Thank you; please bring them.	Thākur fir (or tāk) Kurisō vel ath Kwawma meth.
How long will you be away?	Kwā lengi verthidh fīr (thīeth, when speaking to more than one) bŭrtū?
We shall come back after riding six hours.	Vīeth Kwawmim āftur eftarath hāver rēdhith īsechstūna.
Where is Reykir?	Kwāreru Rēikir?
You are not going the right way.	Thīer fārith eki rēhtir lēdh.
You must go back a little way.	Thīer verdhith afara til paka taulitith.

Our young Icelandic student was very proud of the native Sagas, and justly so. They are works p. 74 highly esteemed, and of interest to the scholar, embodying the history of the Island, tales of its former chiefs, their laws, their feuds, their adoption of Christianity, the sittings of the Althing, great volcanic eruptions, handed down by word of mouth from generation to generation, until the pastors and learned men committed them to manuscript. They are also full of the most romantic adventures, stirring incidents, and courageous assaults, dear to the heart of every Icelander, and treasured by them as a record of their country's history and its people's hardihood.

Icelandic Farm. Cod fish drying. *Etched by F.P. Fellows, from a sketch by the Author*, 1888.
p. 75

CHAPTER VII.
REYKIR.

On arriving at Reykir, our guide conducted us to his own dwelling, a fair-sized farm, where he and his wife resided with all their mutual relations, this being the custom in Iceland. In this case they included the wife, her father, mother, grandfather, and sister on the one side; the husband, his two brothers, sister, and mother on the other. Quite a happy little community, as the couple themselves were also blessed with several children.

On entering we were shown into the guest chamber, a small, neatly-furnished apartment, panelled with wood, and containing two windows, neither of which were made to open—a peculiarity not only to be found in Iceland but in some other places, especially in Tyrol. A wooden bedstead stood in one corner, covered with an elaborate patch-work quilt, whilst a table and two chairs constituted the remainder of the furniture. As our party numbered five, some pack boxes were added—not very soft seats after a long jolting ride. A looking-glass hung on the wall; but what a glass! It was quite impossible to recognise your own face in it; I can only liken its reflection to p. 76 what one would see in a kitchen spoon—not a silver spoon—for there the features, though distorted, would be visible, here they were not. Certainly if such mirrors are the only medium of reflection the people of Reyker possess, they will not grow vain of their personal attractions. The room also contained a barometer and an accordion. In most of the houses we entered we found the latter instrument, which the people, being fond of music, amuse themselves with during the long winter evenings. Curiously enough, there is little or no native music, however. A bookcase on the wall contained quite a small library of Icelandic literature.

Tired with our long ride, we were very glad to rest awhile, while our student friend, our guide, and all the combined families in the house down to the babies and the dogs, stood around us, until the room was so full I don't think another soul could have found entrance.

The Icelanders are on first acquaintance with strangers somewhat reserved; but if treated affably this reserve soon wears off, and their hospitality is unbounded. Even among the poorest a night's lodging is never refused to a traveller.

In outlying districts the farmhouses take the place of inns, whilst the charges are on a most moderate scale.

We brought with us some cheese and biscuits, and a pound of Buzzard's chocolate, which the farmer's wife supplemented with coffee and 'skyr,' the latter served in soup plates. p. 77

Skyr is the national dish, taking the place of porridge to a Scotchman, and is nothing less than curded sheep's milk, like German 'dicke-milch,' eaten with sugar, to which cream is added as a luxury. As it was rather sour, we fought shy of it at first, fearing future consequences, but this was unnecessary. It is really excellent, and the natives eat it in large quantities. Huge barrels of this skyr are made during the time the sheep are in full milk, and stored away for winter's use. It is agreeable to the taste, satisfying, and wholesome.

While eating our lunch, our host and his numerous family circle—who all seemed much interested at our presence—did nothing but ply us with continual questions about England, the English people, and the cost of the various articles we either wore or carried with us.

We invited our host and one or two of his friends to taste our cheese and chocolate, when after every mouthful they each shook hands with all the gentlemen of our party; whilst those of the women who shared our repast, after shaking hands with the gentlemen, kissed Miss T. and myself most affectionately.

Class distinction is unknown in Iceland; in fact, there are no gentry, in our acceptation of the term, and little or no wealth among the inhabitants.

I believe the Bishop is the richest man in the Island, and his income is about £150 a year, a sum which these simple-minded folk look upon as riches.

Our coffee and skyr, with attendance for seven p. 78 people, cost 1s. 7½d. , a sum reasonable enough to meet any traveller's purse.

At the ports, however, in Iceland as elsewhere, we found we had to keep our wits about us to avoid being cheated, the English being credited as made of money.

Near to this farmhouse, at Reykir, there were some hot springs which we visited, and we stood and watched with much interest the water bubbling up to the surface.

Close to one of these springs we noticed a large open tub in which the family washing was being done in the natural hot water thus supplied; but the water was yellow, and gave off a sulphureous odour—although it did not seem to discolour the clothes.

The ground around the house was, as usual, piled up with dried fish. It is difficult to realise the stench caused by this food supply, unless one has experienced it. Cod liver oil is made in large quantities in Iceland, and exported to England, where it is then refined for use. If a lover of cod liver oil—and I believe such eccentric persons exist—could once be placed within 500 yards of its manufacture, I feel sure they would never taste it again.

Our guide was one of the largest farmers in Iceland, and owned the adjoining island, namely, 'Lonely Island,' or 'Drangey,' famous as the retreat of the outlawed hero of the 'Gretter-Saga. ' The legend states that one Christmas night the chief's fire went out, and having no means of rekindling p. 79 it, he swam from Drangey Island to the Reykir farm to get a light, a distance which to us, humanly speaking, seems impossible for any man to have done.

The tale goes on to say that an old witch went out in a boat to visit Gretter on Drangey. The boat upset and she was drowned; but a large rock like a boat in full sail rose from the sea a few yards from the Island itself.

The 'Saga' contains many wonderful tales in connection with this locality, specially relative to the high table-land which rises almost perpendicularly above the sea. The scenery in this part of the Island is very fine. On the west side of the 'Skagaffiryr,' a fair-sized river, are seen the peaks of the 'Tindastoll,' a very steep range of mountains intersected with water-worn gorges; while opposite, 'Malmey,' or 'Sandstone Isle,' juts into the sea, north of a rude peninsula with a low isthmus that appears almost like an island.

Drangey from Reykir. Aug. 9th, 1886.

In the middle of this fjord Drangey is situated. This island, which was the property of our guide, is a huge mass of rock, nearly perpendicular, while at p. 80 one end is the witch's rock resembling the ship in full sail. Drangey is the home of innumerable eider-ducks, who swim at will in and about the surrounding waters. The drake is a very handsome bird, a large portion of his plumage being white; the hen is smaller, and brown in colour. In disposition the birds are very shy and retiring. The hen builds her nest with down plucked from her own breast; this nest the farmer immediately takes possession of; the poor bird makes a second in like manner, which is likewise confiscated; the third nest he leaves untouched, for by this time the bird's breast is almost bare. Eider-down is very valuable, fetching from 12s. to 20s. per pound. When the farmer desires to catch the eider-duck, he places on the shore, at low water, a small board, carefully set with a series of snares on its surface, and as the birds walk over it they are made prisoners by their feet. There must have been many thousands of eider-duck between Reykir and Drangey, and no gun is allowed to be fired for miles around.

Owing to the uneven nature of the ground, caused by constant earth mounds, even where the soil is good the plough is used with great difficulty. In fact, it can only be utilised by removing the sod and levelling the earth with a spade, until smooth enough for a pony to drag the plough over it. There are very few ploughs, or indeed any farming implements of any size in Iceland, the farmers being too poor to buy them, nor are the latter at all an enterprising class, contenting them p. 81 selves with the primitive method of cultivating the soil which their forefathers used to adopt. Our guide being a man of more energy than his brethren, and wealthier, had invested in a plough, of which he was very proud, and exhibited to us as a great novelty, evidently thinking we had never seen such a wonderful thing.

Hay was being cut all the time we were in the Island, cut under every possible disadvantage, and yet cut with marvellous persistency. With this labour, of course, the frost mounds interfere, being most disastrous to the scythe, and yet the natives never leave a single blade of grass, cutting round and round, and between these curious little hillocks. On the hay crop so very much depends, for when that fails, ponies die, sheep and cattle have to be killed and the meat preserved, and the farmer is nearly ruined. Hay is therefore looked upon as a treasure to its possessor, and is most carefully stored for the cattle's winter provender; but as during the greater part of the year the Icelanders are snowed up, the cultivation of hay or cereals is a difficult matter.

In many parts of Iceland there exist enormous stretches of country covered with dangerous bog, which are, of course, at present undrained. Now, however, that an Agricultural College has been established in the Island, it is hoped a fresh impetus will be given to farming operations in general. At present there are only about 220 acres under cereal cultivation, whilst its inhabitants number over 70,000! Although there are no trees, as before p. 82 said, there is no scarcity of flowers, indeed the flora is particularly rich, in some instances being composed of specimens not found elsewhere. Often for miles the ground is thickly carpeted with the most beautiful mountain and Arctic flowers, sometimes nestling even in the snow, which lies in patches quite near to the towns. Iceland moss is found on the lava plains.

Mr Gordon was a botanist, and brought home a large collection of specimens; many more, on which he had set great store, were unfortunately lost from the pony's back. The following is a list of those he secured, a great number of which we found growing among huge boulders in high barren places.

LIST OF PLANTS BROUGHT FROM ICELAND.

1. Plantago maritima.
2. Raniunculus acris.
3. Euphrasia officinalis.
4. Alchemilla vulgaris.
5. Do. alpina.
6. Erigeron alpinus.
7. Rumex acetosa.
8. Do. acetocella.
9. Myosotis sylvatica. (?)
10. Cardamine pratensis.
11. Comarum palustris.
12. Trifolium repens.
13. Saxifraga oppositifolia.
14. Empetrum nigrum.
15. Cerastium alpinum.
16. Cynoglossum officinale. (?)
17. Penguicula vulgaris.
18. Poa alpina.
19. Capsella bursa pastoris.
39. Parnassia palustris.
40. Cerastium vulgatum.
20. Galium saxatile.
21. Stellaria aquatica.
22. Eriocaulon vaginatum.
23. Dryas octopetale.
24. Salix herbacea.
25. Do. lapponica.
26. Do. aurita.
27. Polygonum viviperum.
28. Thalictrum alpinum.
29. Leontodon taraxacum.
30. Samolus valerandi.
31. Equisetum pratense.
32. Stellaria cerastoides.
33. Viola tricolor.
34. Do. palustris.
35. Cerastium trigynum.
36. Potentilla reptans.
37. Arabis. (sp. ?)
38. Betula nana. p. 83
46. Potentilla anserina.
47. Aparagia hispidus.
41. Silene acaulis.
42. Vaccinium uliginosum.
43. Do. vitis idea.
44. Thymus serpyllifolia.
45. Gentiana campestris.
48. Rhinanthus crista galli.
49. Galium vulgaris.
50. Galium parisiense.
51. Geranium pratense.

Names furnished by C. A. Gordon, M.D. C.B.

Birch 2 species.   } included
Willow 3 "   in above.

Mushrooms grow abundantly in Iceland, and we much enjoyed them, eaten with salt, as a supplement to our meals.

After some hours' rest at Reykir, we remounted, and rode back to Sauderkrok, parting with much regret from our student friend, who had proved a most agreeable and intelligent addition to our party.

That night we were none of us sorry to exchange our saddles for our berths in the *Camoens*, having been on horseback the greater part of the day, on a road the roughness of which is indescribable.

A further steam of twelve hours up the Hruta Fjord brought us to Bordeyri, a still smaller place than Sauderkrok. Here our captain informed us he should have to wait thirty-six hours for the discharge of further cargo. This fjord is very dangerous, for it has never been surveyed, consequently deep-sea leads were frequently used, the sailors meanwhile chanting a very pretty refrain. When we anchored opposite Bordeyri, we all p. 84 noticed the anxious look which the captain's face had lately worn had left him, and how pleased he seemed to have brought his steamer safely to her moorings.

We landed in a boat which came alongside the *Camoens*, and commenced at once to take a survey of the place. A few dozen houses or so, with a large store, where every necessary of life was supposed to be procurable (at least an Icelander's necessities), constituted the town. We entered the store in search of some native curiosities to carry home. A brisk trade was being carried on in sugar candy, large sacks of which were purchased by the farmers, who had come to meet the steamer and barter their goods for winter supplies. Never was any shopping done under greater difficulties than our own, and we almost despaired of making ourselves understood. The store-man, however, grinned most good-naturedly when we failed to do so, and we at last unearthed some finely-carved drinking-horns, and a couple of powder flasks, which we thought would help to decorate a London hall.

While at Bordeyri, we felt we were the subject of much amusement and admiration among the little crowd of natives who flocked to see us, forming also, I doubt not, a topic of conversation among them for many a day to come.

Our survey of the town was soon made, so we ordered ponies for a ride up country, this being the best way of passing our time. On the way p. 85 we saw a number of large ravens; splendid birds they were and wonderfully tame; the ground was quite covered in places by flocks of them.

Iceland boasts of a great variety of birds; in fact, they form an attraction to many English sportsmen to visit the Island. Both my brother and A. L. T. were sportsmen, but our time was too limited to admit of the exercise of this taste. Among the birds may be noted swan, geese, duck, curlew, mallard, snipe, plover, ptarmigan,—90 species of birds, in fact, 54 of which are wildfowl. During our ride, A. L. T. shot a fine raven, and on our return to the ship, my brother skinned and stuffed it, as a memento of his inland trip. Many of the passengers were so interested in his performance, that he was called on to deliver a lecture on skinning and stuffing birds, and he explained how skilfully this could be accomplished, with the help of a penknife alone. On another occasion, A. L. T. caught a baby curlew as yet unable to fly, but the cries of the parents as they whirled round and round us seeking their offspring, were so heart-rending, that in sheer pity he placed the little thing back on the ground, where it was instantly joined by the old birds, who uttered cries of delight, which we continued hearing until we were well out of sight.

There are great attractions for sportsmen in Iceland—reindeer shooting on the western side of the Island, whale and seal shooting, and salmon and trout fishing, the latter being met with in all p. 86 the rivers. Indeed some of the finest salmon fishing in the world is to be found here, and several Englishmen rent rivers, where they enjoy this sport every summer; the life being free and independent, the expenses small, and the sport excellent, naturally form many attractions. At the same time, so much netting and trapping of the fish goes on, there is every probability the salmon will be exterminated before long.

Our ride out of Bordeyri was very interesting. There are some hot springs on the east of the fjord, which are reached by boat, but which we had not time to visit. Had we remained longer, we should much have liked to see the 'Anglica fish-lakes,' but these were a full day's journey from Bordeyri, and quite out of our route. They are, we were told, abundantly stocked with char, trout, and other good fish, and afford an excellent halting-place for sporting travellers.

A part of our way lay along a peat-track, over which we raced our ponies, varying our exploits later amid bogs, which required the most careful riding to avoid a catastrophe. As usual, there were many rivers to be forded, through which our ponies plodded up to their middles, never flinching even at the coldest glacial water. Often during our rides, towards evening the cold became intense, although for a few hours about mid-day the sun was very hot.

Hruta Fjord, Borderyre, Iceland, Aug. 11, 1886. *Etched by Frank P. Fellows, from a sketch by the Author*, 1888. *Page 86*.

After some hours' riding, we arrived at another typical farm, which I sketched from my pony's p. 87 back. The farmhouse, and a small hamlet of wooden huts which lay around it, formed a good foreground to the distant fjord. Dismounting, we entered the house by a low door, knocking our heads against the rafters as we traversed a long dark passage which led to the guest-chamber. This room, as usual, was neatly panelled with wood, and contained a bed, chairs, etc., but, from the absence of fresh air, was fearfully close. Our ride had sharpened our appetite, and we at once produced our lunch supply, consisting of cheese and biscuits, etc. We offered some of the biscuits to the farmer, who at first turned them round and round in his hand suspiciously, then seeing that we ate them with enjoyment, he raised one solemnly to his lips, tasted it, and then speedily devoured his share of the meal. In a short time all the various members of the family joined us, and, *sans cérémonie*, proceeded to examine our belongings. Pipes, match-boxes, watches, furs, and jewellery were all passed in review, and we were asked the price of each article, and whether we had brought them out from England. Our table knives seemed to cause them the greatest astonishment, and as the Sheffield steel glanced in the sun, they were quite childlike in their delight; certainly our English cutlery was a great contrast to the jagged iron knives which served them at table. In our turn, we admired their quaint old silver ornaments, but when we testified a desire to purchase, we failed to meet with any response. p. 88

We did not, as first proposed, remain the night at this farm, its accommodation not being sufficiently enticing, so our hostess was saved fulfilling the curious Icelandic custom considered a compliment to strangers, of putting all her guests to bed herself, whether man or woman, and not leaving the room until they were safely tucked up. We cannot say, however, we encountered this form of hospitality ourselves, but we were told it was constantly carried out.

As we sat round the table at our meal

in this faraway region, so distant from all the trammels of Society, we wondered what expressions the faces of our London friends would have worn could they have seen our party passing the only spoon available from one person to the other, occasionally even eating with our fingers. Certainly our surroundings were much at variance with a well-appointed luncheon table, and yet we enjoyed ourselves all the more from its primitive simplicity. Lunch over, we prepared to continue our journey, but found our ponies had wandered much further off than usual, and our guide went to seek them.

The Icelander and his pony have initiated signs, which serves them in lieu of language. For instance, when the rider dismounts, and simply leaves the reins over the animal's head, the latter knows that he will be wanted again soon, and must not wander far off; if, on the other hand, the bridle is left loose, the pony knows he may roam at will in search of food until his master seeks him. p. 89

We rode back to Bordeyri, which we reached in the evening, and again slept on board the *Camoens*. During our absence up country the previous day we heard that the ship's company had been in a great state of excitement, consequent on the embarkation of some forty emigrants from Bordeyri and its surrounding neighbourhood. We saw these our fellow-passengers the next day, men, women, and children, many of the former quite old, apparently not more than one in five appeared capable of a good day's work. These emigrants were bound for Manitoba and Winnipeg, in each of which places there is an Icelandic colony, and which settlements they could reach at a cost of £6, 10s. per head. Poor things! we wondered if they had taken into serious consideration the difficulties that lay in their path in the New World they were seeking. Probably, considering the land they were leaving was one of volcanoes and desert wastes, they hoped for better things. Their Icelandic life must indeed be hard and colourless, so hard as to have taken from them all pleasure in existence. To judge by their apathy, these questions did not seem to have been taken much into account by them; possibly when the sight of green fields, and Nature's abundance, break upon their view, dormant will, and energy may rise to fresh surroundings, and inspire them with an impetus to work.

Ah! speculate as we would upon their future, and probably we did so more than they did them p. 90 selves, all we could do for them was to wish them God-speed and good luck in their venture.

A bright 12th of August dawned at sea as we left the Hruta Fjord, and steamed again towards the Arctic Circle and Cape North. When we met at breakfast the conversation naturally turned upon grouse, and 12th of August sport in general, and the gentlemen wished themselves in Scotland, and exchanged their last year's experiences there. I remembered mine also, for I was staying in a country house in Lanarkshire, and some dozen men ready equipped for sport stood staring out of the windows of the breakfast-room, grumbling lustily at the pouring rain, and finally having to abandon their shooting expedition for the day, and content themselves with dancing Scotch reels, and otherwise amusing 'we girls,'—sorry consolation for the 12th of August!

The day wore on, and we had the unusual treat of a calm sea, but as the wind blew straight across from the ice regions, it was fearfully cold, pack-ice being seen in the distance, whilst an hour or so later we were enveloped in a thick fog.

The captain looked uneasy, as he had discerned ice ahead, and during his last voyage this fog had betokened its dangerous proximity. To turn back now and go round the Island to Reykjavik would be a serious loss of time. We slackened speed, the fog-horn was blown, and several times the sailors took deep-sea soundings.

Snaefell Jökull—Iceland—Aug 13. 1886, 11 P.M. *Etched by Frank P Fellows from a sketch by the Author.* 1888.

Reikjavik, Chief town of Iceland. *Reduced & etched from a Photograph by F.P. Fellows.* 1888.

At dinner-time the captain handed me a parcel p. 91 containing a tiny shell and a piece of coal black lava, drawn up from 66 fathoms of water S.-E. North Cape, and 27 miles from the same. Though only 10 miles from land, the fog so entirely hid the coast that we missed one of the prettiest views of Iceland.

The next day, however, was lovely, and under a cloudless blue sky the coast-line showed to the greatest advantage. The sunset that night was one of the finest I have ever seen. Snaefell Jökull, with its snow summit, stood out against the most perfect sky, the colours deepening from yellow to orange, and vermilion to carmine, and constantly changing, like a kaleidoscope.

At 11.30 p.m. the sun had not set, but was illuminating the heavens with the most gorgeous colouring, reminding one of the distant warmer regions of the south, although at the same time the thermometer stood far below freezing point as we steamed within the Arctic Circle.

p. 92

CHAPTER VIII.

REYKJAVIK.

Reykjavik is the capital of Iceland. It has a population of about 4000, and is pleasantly situated on the shores of a small bay to the north of a headland, which forms an excellent harbour. Several islands lie so close to the shore that they can be reached on foot at low water. We had anchored here at night, and when we left our berths in the morning, the town looked quite imposing as compared with the smaller ones we had already seen.

We were somewhat disappointed to hear from the captain that he could not remain a minute longer than four days at Reykjavik, possibly only three and a half, during which time, in order to pay our visit to the Geysers (the chief attraction in our trip), we should be obliged to ride 160 miles over very rough ground; and even calculating our riding powers at 40 miles a day, no time would be left for contingencies, or a visit to Hecla, which had been an object of our ambition.

It was, however, a question of being contented to see what we could in that time, or remaining in Iceland for the next steamer, a disaster we did not p. 93 look forward to at all, as we had heard of travellers who had been left for weeks at Reykjavik, from failing to present themselves on board at the appointed time. Vaughan and Mr Gordon were up early, and went ashore before breakfast, carrying an introduction to 'Herr Zoega,' the chief guide and pony owner in the capital; and they engaged for our excursion to the Geysers twenty good ponies and two guides, one of whom could speak English, at the same time bringing back on board four pack boxes to fill with eatables and such necessary clothing as we required for the trip. These boxes we packed as tightly as possible, so as to prevent the things rattling about on the ponies' backs. They were about 18 inches long, 12 deep, and some 8 inches wide, consequently the necessary luggage for five of us quite filled two of them, notwithstanding that we took as little as possible.

Our provender consisted of potted meats, half a ham, biscuits, beer, and whisky, and with dinner utensils, such as enamelled metal plates, tumblers, knives, forks, etc., from our luncheon basket, quite filled the boxes. To carry one's own food on such an excursion is absolutely necessary, unless you can live on coffee and skyr.

When calculating the number of ponies to be hired, you must allow two per head, whether for riders or for luggage, as from the rough nature of the ground the animals soon tire, and frequent changes are necessary.

A tent had also to be sought for and hired, and p. 94 while this was being found, and our ponies laden, and rugs and mackintoshes strapped on to our riding steeds, we were told by our guide that at least two hours must elapse before they would be ready for us to start, so we decided to see what we could of the town meanwhile.

The principal buildings—none of which were of any architectural beauty—were the Cathedral, the Senate House, the Hospital, and the College.

I must not forget to mention the Gaol, the only one in the Island. It is unlike any other I ever heard of, as it very rarely has an inmate! Honesty amongst the people themselves is wonderful, and murder is almost unknown.

Near the Cathedral, on a grassy space in the centre of the town, stood a monument to Albert Thorwaldsen, the sculptor, who was of Icelandic descent, although, I believe, claimed by Denmark, as one of her gifted sons. Reykjavik also boasts a small Antiquarian Museum, which, strange to say, is to be found in the Senate House, and for the size of the town (4000 inhabitants) there is a good Free Library, in a loft under the roof of the Cathedral.

We were pointed out a really interesting sight in the Cathedral-a rude wooden crucifix, which had been discovered in a lava cave, and is believed to be a Chaldean relic. There was also a collection of 13th century ecclesiastical garments and enamelled crucifixes. In the adjoining Museum we saw a number of weapons of war dating from the 4th p. 95 century, as well as rare old drinking-cups of walrus ivory, beautifully carved, and some old-fashioned tapestry. Some of the old silver ornaments were really quaint, and the carving on the flat-irons much interested me, as I had never seen so many or such fine ones before.

In the library is the first Bible printed in Iceland, at Holar, in 1584; also a very curious work on 'Magic;' two old versions of the New Testament, dated 1540; whilst its shelves boasted quite a large collection of modern works on all subjects.

There are two small inns in the town, as well as a club house, post office, and stores, besides a druggist, a photographer, and two or three silversmiths. As to vehicles, there were none, and the silence of the streets reminded one of Venice.

Tradition says that the town was founded in 877, by one 'Tugolfi,' a Norse settler. The early Icelandic settlers are reputed to have had a curious mode of determining the spot on which they should build their homes. On approaching the coast, the head of a family threw overboard the pillars on which the seat of honour in his former home had been raised, and wherever these pillars floated ashore, there he believed the gods of his ancestors wished him to erect his new dwelling-place.

Tugolfi's high seat pillars had drifted into 'Reykjavik Bay,' consequently he there took up his abode, and thus laid the foundation of the only prosperous town in Iceland. p. 96

Our time was too limited to visit many stores in Reykjavik in search of curios, but being possessed with the idea that some good old silver articles were to be obtained here, we tried our best to find them. But the idea turned out to be an illusion, for after inquiring at three of the shops, the only things we succeeded in finding were two silver buckles, for which, after much bargaining, we paid 39s. each; certainly not cheap, but they served us as mementoes of Reykjavik.

We had brought ashore a parcel of letters, which we carried to the post office for despatch, but learnt that they would go no sooner than ourselves in the *Camoens*. As there was a great possibility of our not returning from our trip to the Geysers in time to catch the steamer, we left our letters, in order that folks at home might receive some news of us if we failed to reappear at the appointed time, and suggested therein we might be detained. In such a case, we should have been obliged to wait for a Danish boat, which would touch at the capital in about a fortnight's time.

While we were gleaning this information, Vaughan had been asked by a Scotchman (the husband of our ship's companion in the brown silk) to go and see his son. He and the boy had ridden from Akureyri to Reykjavik, while we steamed round the Island. The poor boy, while resting his pony near the mud springs, had run off to see them nearer, when suddenly the earth gave way, and one leg was in boiling mud to the knee, and the p. 97 other immersed above the ankle. Luckily his father was near, and extricated him; but for that, and the fact of his wearing high riding boots, he might have been burnt to death, or lamed for life—as it was, the boiling mud had burnt the boots through before they could be pulled off, and the knee above had been severely hurt. Nothing could be done but ride on, and the brave little chap managed to stick on his pony, although in awful pain, until he reached home a day and a half later.

My brother suggested all he could think of to alleviate his suffering, and, when we returned from the Geysers, had the pleasure of finding his little patient very much better, though likely to remain a cripple for a considerable length of time.

At a bookseller's in Reykjavik, we procured an Icelandic translation of an English book by one of our standard authors, selecting it from a number of well-known works, such as Shakespear, Scott, Byron, Dean Stanley, John Stuart Mill, George Eliot, etc., all of which stood in long rows, translated into the Norse tongue. We also carried off a neat little Icelandic newspaper, printed in the capital; but, unfortunately, not one of our party could decipher its contents.

This little newspaper had been printed after our arrival in the *Camoens*, and furnished the only news the Icelanders had of the outside world since the advent of a Danish ship a fortnight previously. Iceland has not yet been annexed by cable, and knows nothing of the marvellous scien p. 98 tific invention which now flashes news so quickly round our world.

The hour was now approaching when our caravan was to make its start for the Geysers, so we returned to the town. Here the landlord's daughter, at our request, exhibited herself in her *fête* attire, in which she made a quaint and pretty picture. The dress consisted of a thickly-pleated black silk skirt, very full and somewhat short, embroidered round the bottom with a deep band of gold thread; a black bodice, also similarly embroidered with gold down the front and round the collar; a handsome necklet and girdle of silver gilt, and a high headdress of white muslin, in appearance resembling a Normandy cap. This, she told us, she always wore on Sundays and great occasions, dressing like an Englishwoman on week days.

We found our ponies all in readiness at the appointed hour, and our excitement may be imagined when we caught sight of our cavalcade, with its appendages, drawn up in order before the so-called hotel, for our former excursions were as nothing compared to the undertaking which now lay before us, and we realised that all our energy would be required for the enterprise.

Behold our party, then. Two ladies and three gentlemen; two guides, one being employed as pony-driver; seven ponies for riding, and seven for changing on the road; three pack ponies, two laden with our luggage, and one p. 99 with tents; and three unladen ponies for exchange weights: twenty in all, a goodly company of quadrupeds, well selected and sure-footed. The ponies, too, besides being picked ones for the work, were well 'trapped,' and newly shod, with the saddles, girths, straps, and buckles all in order. So at least 'Zoega' told us, with an assurance that we might depend on his forethought, adding that if we ladies could really accomplish the 160 miles' ride in three and a half days, his ponies should not be found lacking, but he had never yet known any lady do it under five, and he did not think we knew what rough riding lay before us. Miss T—— and myself, not daunted by the difficulties presented, made up our minds, if possible, to compass the ride, see the 'Geysers,' and be back at Reykjavik in time to catch the steamer, for we had no mind to be left in Iceland another fortnight; so we laughingly told Zoega we would show him what English ladies could do in the way of riding, and he might expect to see us back on the appointed day.

Up we all mounted, to the amusement of the crowd, which had collected round the cavalcade. The words, 'Are you ready?' were quickly answered by 'Yes;' but when one of the bye-standers saw we ladies were furnished only with men's saddles, there was quite a commotion. 'The ladies will never be able to ride all that way in that fashion; only native women can ride so, not p. 100 real ladies,' and so terrible did they make out the prospect of the road, that we were persuaded to take two wretchedly uncomfortable side-saddles with us as far as Thingvalla, which we never used, far preferring our own arrangement.

That start from Reykjavik was a memorable one. It was a glorious morning, the outcome of a splendid sunset the previous night, and the air so genial and warm that for the first time since we set foot on the Island we dispensed with our furs.

A picturesque party we made as we rode on our way towards Thingvalla, a stretch of seven hours' hard riding, one of the guides and Vaughan driving before them the thirteen loose ponies. These were not attached to each other, but followed the leader, and went very well, only now and then one or two strayed from the path, when down jumped the guide, ran after them, and with a curious shriek brought them back in line. Our guides were most dexterous riders, and proved also most kind and attentive. Their names were Signithur Sigurthsen and Jon Eriksen. We had been cautioned that if treated with hauteur the guides often became sullen, whilst kindness ensured their devotion and courtesy, and as we never tried the former tone, we were capital friends with them.

The guidebooks had led us to believe that after we had left Reykjavik a mile or so we should find no roads whatever. This is strictly p. 101 true, as there are no made roads, but here and there we came across long stretches of level land

and peat, where we could get really a good gallop, whilst on the other hand there were many parts of our route where no beast could go faster than a walk, and others which only a mule or an Icelandic pony could compass.

A road or bridle path is being constructed between Akureyri and Reykjavik, and some 20 miles is already roughly made, although it will probably take years to complete.

Herr Zoega had certainly been as good as his word, and supplied us with excellent ponies, some of which excelled in trotting, some in cantering, and others in pacing, but the latter motion was very trying, and I always objected to mounting those which had been trained to pace.

The Icelandic fashion of making the pony go fast is to kick its side incessantly with the legs, which a native does for hours together, and so accustomed is the pony to this 'clapping,' that he slackens his pace as soon as it ceases.

The scenery along our route was in many parts very fine and wild in the extreme, huge boulders of lava and rock intersecting our path, and standing like massive ruins on either side, the lava having evidently cooled down in an almost liquid state, and presenting a most uncanny appearance.

Professor Geikie, speaking of the Icelandic volcanoes, says,—

'On several occasions the ashes have fallen so p. 102 thickly between the Orkneys and Shetlands that vessels passing there have had the unwonted deposit shovelled off their decks in the mornings. In the year 1783, during the memorable eruption of Skaptar-Jökull (80 miles east of Hecla), so vast an amount of fine dust was ejected, that the atmosphere over Iceland continued loaded with it for months afterwards. It fell in such quantities over parts of Caithness—a distance of 600 miles—as to destroy the crops. That year is still spoken of by the inhabitants as the year of "the ashie." Traces of the same deposit have been observed in Norway, and even as far as Holland.' .

The most stupendous outpouring of lava on record was that which took place from the Skaptar-Jökull.

'Preceded by violent earthquakes all along the southern coast, it burst out with great fury, drying up the river in twenty-four hours, and filling its bed. The lava in some places was 600 feet deep and 200 wide, flowing like a mighty river towards the sea, wrapping whole districts in flames, re-melting old lavas, opening subterranean caverns, one of its streams reaching the ocean. It was in full activity for two and a half months, and did not entirely cease for six months.

'It took the lava more than two years to cool. One stream was 50 miles long, 12 to 15 broad on the plain, and from 1 to 600 feet deep; another was 40 miles long, and 7 wide. Pasture lands 100 miles around were destroyed by the pumice sand p. 103 and ashes. The matter ejected has been estimated as twice the volume of Mount Hecla, or one hundred thousand millions cubic yards, probably as large as any single mass of the older igneous rocks known to exist—according to Bischoff, greater than the bulk of Mount Blanc.

'Man, his cattle, houses, churches and grass lands were burnt up, noxious vapours filled the air, and the earth was shrouded by clouds of ashes.' .

A few instances of the actual outbreak of a submarine eruption have been witnessed. In the early summer of 1783 a volcanic eruption took place about 30 miles from Cape Reykjanaes, on the west coast. An island was thrown up from which fire and smoke continued to issue, but in less than a year the waves had washed the loose pumice away, leaving a submerged reef from 5 to 30 fathoms below sea level. About a month later followed the frightful outbreak of Skaptar-Jökull, a distance of nearly 200 miles from this submarine vent.

The bluest of skies was above our heads, and the atmosphere so clear we could see objects many miles distant, among them 'Hecla,' whose snowy cap glistened like silver in the sun.

The air was so pure and invigorating, that it acted like champagne on all our party, and we were in the highest spirits.

About every two hours we halted and gave our ponies a brief rest, letting them nibble the short grass near, when any such was to be found, then changing our saddles to the backs of the reserve animals we started afresh, the p. 104 wild mountain paths becoming steeper and rougher as we advanced.

We had only passed two farms on our way, and our guide informing us there was not another for many miles, feeling very hungry after our long morning's ride, we dismounted by the side of a babbling brook for lunch, and did full justice to the ham and tinned beef we had brought from London with us. While eating our meal, our twenty ponies were allowed to wander at will with the reins thrown over their heads, and had there been any passers-by we might have been taken for a gipsy encampment

Luncheon over, everything had to be washed, and securely packed, but despite all our previous care we found some of our china had been sorely smashed, and the biscuits shaken to perfect powder.

Our guides shared our repast, respectfully taking their seats at a little distance from us, and their delight at tasting our tinned beef and mustard entertained us greatly. The latter stung poor Jon's mouth till the tears ran down his cheeks, but, nothing daunted, he persevered in taking the condiment, till he grew so fond of it as to ask for it with every kind of food, even spreading it on an Albert biscuit.

Hitherto our path had wound over a range of hills amid which we saw several small lakes, and the view looking westward towards 'Snaefell Jökull,' which rises like a pyramid of ice from the sea, was charming. Our lunch had been taken in the valley of the 'Seljadalr,' and now once p. 105 more in our saddles, we followed a bridle-path upwards towards the plateau of 'Mosfellshei,' passing through a wild rocky glen of great natural beauty. The 'Mosfellshei' is a long, stony, dreary waste, several miles in length, so wild and rough as to render riding no easy task, the path leading through dreary tracks of lava, over which the ponies stepped with cat-like agility, hardly if ever stumbling, and going up and down hill as easily as on level ground. After two hours or more of this rough riding, suddenly, at a bend of the hill, we came upon our first view of Thingvalla Lake, and were charmed with it and the surrounding country. It was like going out of a desert into fairyland. The lake, which is 45 miles long, and of a deep cobalt blue, can be seen only in part, as the hills around project to such an extent as to apparently divide the water into a series of lakes, instead of one broad expanse. It was a glorious day with a bright warm sun, and a clear blue sky, and everything around looked fair and peaceful. We were so delighted with the spot, that we stopped to make sketches, allowing the pack ponies to get ahead of us.

Not long after remounting and calmly jogging on our way, we suddenly came upon the verge of a tremendous chasm, which, opening at our feet, divided the barren ground on which we stood, from a lovely sunlit plain of many miles in extent. Winding our way down, we entered the Almannagya by a narrow fissure. The path leads for p. 106 nearly a mile, the rocks rising as perpendicular walls on either side from 80 to 100 feet; so narrow was it in some places that there was little more than room for the path. In other places where it widened, patches of snow still remained.

Here was indeed a halting-place full of interest, and we accordingly dismounted, and prepared to spend some time in lionising a spot so replete with historic records.

Running parallel were two or three such chasms, of minor magnitude, over the less steep parts of which we managed to scramble, before remounting our ponies, which it was necessary to do, although Thingvalla Farm lay but a few yards distant, because of the intervening river, which we had to ford.
p. 107

CHAPTER IX.

THINGVALLA.

Independently of the beauty and natural curiosities of the spot, Thingvalla is so associated with the early history of the Norse people, its government and its laws, that it deserves a longer notice here than has been given to any other of our halting-places.

We had descended into the 'Almannagja' by a steep rocky causeway made between cloven rocks, and reached the narrow islet where, in times gone by, when feudal despotism was the only government acknowledged, the chiefs of the Island met to regulate the affairs of state. Whenever it might have been that the volcanic eruption which had shivered the rocks into their present fissured condition had occurred, it had left this spot so surrounded by deep crevices as to render it impregnable, save by the rude causeway which connected it with the exterior level. This plain was, as already recorded, chosen by the founders of the first Icelandic parliament for their sittings. At the upper end of the plain, we were shown the stone seats which the principal legislators and judges occupied during p. 108 their deliberations. Not far from here lies also the 'Logberg,' or 'law rock,' a large mound from whence the laws were proclaimed or judgments given to the people who assembled on the outside slope of the eastern wall of the rift, in view of the proceedings below. Our notice was likewise directed to the 'blood stone,' on which, for certain offences, the criminals were condemned to have their backs broken, after which barbarous punishment they were hurled backwards, and fell into the chasm below.

In Lord Dufferin's 'Letters from High Latitudes,' he thus describes this spot:—

'Long ago—who shall say how long—some vast commotion had shaken the foundations of the Island, and bubbling up from sources far away amid the inland hills, a fiery deluge must have rushed down between their ridges, until, escaping from the narrower gorges, it found space to spread itself into one broad sheet of molten stone over an entire district of country, reducing its varied surface to one vast blackened level.

'One of two things must then have occurred, either the vitrified mass, contracting as it cooled—the centre area of fifty square miles must have burst asunder at either side from the adjoining plateau, and sunk down to its present level—leaving the two parallel gorges, or chasms, which form its lateral boundaries, to mark the limits of the disruption; or else, while the lava was still in a fluid state, its upper surface became solid, and p. 109 formed a roof beneath, while the mother stream flowing on to lower levels, left a vast cavern into which the upper crust subsequently plumped down "and formed this level plain."'

For three hundred years did the little republic of Iceland hold their parliaments within this romantic precinct, three hundred years of remarkable independence, but during which period Paganism and spiritual darkness prevailed throughout the Island. In the organisation of the first 'Althing,' priestly power predominated, no less than thirty-nine priests having seats. During the early settlement of Iceland, the land was divided into four quarters, each quarter sending its quota of priests to parliament, while each priest thus nominated a member of the Althing, was accompanied by two retainers, or assessors, as they were termed. Inclusive of the President, the Log-men, and its numerous sacerdotal representatives, the members of the Althing are said to have numbered 145 persons.

As we stood by these time-honoured rocks, where in long ages past ancient Norse chieftains had promulgated their laws, we tried to conjure up the scene,—the rocky entrance to this weird spot, guarded by stalwart Norsemen, the stern senators and law-makers sitting in deep thought, or occupied in stormy debate, while the crowd of interested spectators looked down from the stony platform above. We wondered that although these grand old times of feudalism had passed away, no enterprising artist had been found to transfer to canvas p. 110 an historic record of such deep interest, and thus make the scene live again in modern times.

It was in the year 1000, on the 4th of June, that Iceland abandoned Paganism, and accepted Christianity. This great change was principally brought about through the instrumentality of a Pagan priest named Snorri, who, while travelling in Christian lands, had been converted, and on his return had pressed his new convictions on the people of Iceland. Many of these accepting his tenets caused quite a division in the Island, and the Althing was summoned to take into consideration the new views which had been introduced.

Snorri was invited to address the assembly, and explain the principles of his new-found faith. The members of the Althing listened with great attention, evidently much impressed with what they heard, for Snorri spoke with the enthusiastic zeal of a fresh convert.

There were not wanting, however, those among the representatives who resented the introduction into the Island of this new belief, hence the debate, so records the 'Njol-Saga,' waxed warm, when a messenger rushed in and disturbed the council by the alarming news that a stream of lava had burst out at Olfas, and that the priest's dwelling would soon be overrun. On this one of the heathen opponents to Christianity remarked, 'No wonder the gods exhibit their wrath, when such speeches as we have just heard against their power have been permitted.' On this Snorri with great dignity p. 111 rose up, saying, as he pointed to the riven rocks and deep fissures around them, 'At what then were the gods wroth when this lava was molten and overran the whole district upon which we now stand?' To this speech there was no reply, for all well knew that the plain was one of the most remarkable lava tracks in the Island.

It is presumed that Snorri's remark told, and his persuasive eloquence won the day, for shortly after, the Icelanders in a body accepted Christianity as their national faith, and this apparently without either bloodshed or quarrelling.

In the 'Saga' mention is made of many remarkable sittings and debates which took place within the Althing, some of which ended in such animosity between individual members as to be the cause of party feuds and bloodshed.

In connection with the deep rifts which encompass the Althing, a romantic story is told. A Norseman called Flossi, a leader of some conspiracy in the Island, was condemned to death; he evaded this sentence by taking a leap from the blood stone, on which he stood, across the adjoining rift, a feat neither his accusers nor condemners were likely to imitate, and one inspired only by his extreme peril.

In 1800 the Althing was abolished, Iceland having fallen under Danish government; it was re-established again in 1843, but only in a very restricted form, its legislation being cramped in every way by Danish supremacy. In 1845 the p. 112 romantic precinct where the Icelanders held their parliament was abandoned, and the legislative body was removed to the capital of Reykjavik.

In the 'National Encyclopædia,' we found the following note in reference to the new constitution granted to the Icelanders,—

'In 1874, on the occasion of the millennial jubilee of the Island's colonisation, the King of Denmark visited Iceland, and conferred upon his subjects there a new and very liberal constitution, most of its articles being moulded upon the Danish charter of 1849. It conceded to Iceland, in all matters concerning the Island, its own independent legislation and administration, superintended by an assembly, the new Althing consisting of thirty-six members—thirty elected by popular suffrage, and six nominated by the King. It put at the head of the country's affairs a minister named by the King, and residing in Copenhagen, but responsible to the Althing, and exercising his functions through a local governor residing at Reykjavik. It also fully guaranteed the independence of the tribunals, individual freedom, liberty of faith, of the press, of public meetings, the individuality of property, the self-government of principalities, and the equality of all citizens before the law.'

As will clearly be seen, this is a case of Home Rule, though the Icelanders are still in a measure under the Danish Government; apparently much the same kind of legislature as Mr Gladstone is so anxious to confer upon Ireland. The present p. 113 Althing or Parliament has two Houses—an Upper and Lower House; there are twelve members in the former, and twenty-four in the latter. They must all be Icelanders, and usually they sit for about six years. We peeped into the Parliament House during the short time we were in Reykjavik; it was then sitting, but much as I should like to have remained and listened to the proceedings, the odours in the gallery in which we were placed forbade it. The impression it made upon me was that it resembled a small English law-court, the governor sitting in uniform at the head of the Council.

Certainly the ancient mode of transacting affairs of state was a far more interesting one, and the precincts of its primitive Parliament House and law-courts were unrivalled in their rocky architecture and romantic scenery.

Not far from the Almannagya is a very picturesque fall, formed by the waters of the 'Oxara,' which leap in a single bound from an elevation west of the 'Thingfields,' or 'speaking-place' into the 'Almannagya,' flowing through a gap in the rocks, and again leaping into the plain below, forming a large pool.

In this pool it is said in olden times women convicted of witchcraft or infanticide used to be drowned.

Altogether the halt we made at the Thingfields interested us deeply, and the landscape was charming in the extreme. High mountains guard three sides of the plain; among these we had pointed out to us the 'Sular Range,' the dark peaks of the 'Armammsfell,' and the lower ridge of the 'Jornkliff,' p. 114 below, on the north-east of the snow-capped 'Skjaldbreid,' and the peaks of 'Tindjjalla-jökull' with the more distant 'Langjökull' sparkling like silver. South-west of the lake there is another group of mountains seen, from one of which—Hengill—a cloud of steam ascends, it being evidently volcanic. Among the rocks of the 'Almannagya' we saw some pretty mountain sheep grazing, the only sign of life in this wild region. The Icelandic sheep are very small, and we noticed often wander in pairs, one black and one white: they mostly have horns; the wool of the white sheep is spotless. There are plenty of sheep in the Island, and it is for them as much as the ponies that the grass is cut, dried, and stacked under such woeful disadvantages and in such a marvellously painstaking manner.

Thingvalla Parsonage, Iceland, Aug. 14, 1886. *Etched by F. P. Fellows, from a sketch by the Author*, 1888. *Page 114* . Leaving the rift, and crossing over a small river, we arrived at the door of Thingvalla Parsonage. Here it was arranged we were to pass the night. The farms and inns are so few and far between in Iceland, that the parsonages are thrown open for the accommodation of travellers. Formerly the wooden benches of the Thingvalla Church itself used to be converted into sleeping-berths; travellers, however, behaved so indecorously within the sacred walls, that the Bishop forbade the further use of the edifice for this purpose. The church, a simple wooden building, is surrounded by a graveyard, a few iron crosses marking some of the graves. The pulpit dates from 1683, and there is an ancient altar-piece of the Last Supper. The so-called village of p. 115 Thingvalla consists merely of the church, the parsonage, and a few out-houses for storing winter supplies. When we arrived at the parsonage, we learnt that the clergyman was absent,— further, that a party of travellers from our ship had arrived a few hours before us, and had engaged rooms, the only remaining accommodation being two very small bedrooms, and one sitting-room. To Miss T. and myself was assigned the clergyman's own bedroom. This contained the smallest bed I have ever seen, and having to be made available for two persons, we did not pass a very comfortable night. The only luxury in the room was a well-stored bookcase containing many standard works in various languages. Our three gentlemen occupied the remaining bed and sitting-room.

We ascertained that the party who had preceded us consisted of seven men, who having only one bedroom and a small sitting-room, had most of them to sleep on the floor rolled up in their rugs. These men it appeared were not accustomed to the saddle, and having ridden forty miles on the day they arrived at the parsonage, found themselves so stiff on the morrow as to be barely able to continue their journey; indeed, two of their party gave in, and never reached the 'Geysers' at all.

Among the ancient curios of the Thingvalla Parsonage was an old grinding-machine, such as one reads of in the Bible; at this a girl sat turning its stone wheel with her hand, whilst the corn thus converted into flour fell into a receptacle below. In p. 116 all the domestic arrangements Icelanders are very primitive, but this operation was, I think, about the most so of any I witnessed. A large jar containing rice attracted my attention, and curiously enough the rice was not to eat but to make poultices of, instead of linseed. We found the commissariat at the parsonage at a very low ebb; in fact, nothing but coffee and skyr were procurable; and but for our provision of tinned meats we should have fared badly.

We could not even procure white bread, simply the black 'pumpernickel' bread so much prized in Germany. Vaughan persuaded a man to go to the lake and secure us some fish for the next morning's breakfast; this he did, and returned with some excellent pink trout, and yellow char, which we much enjoyed.

No one at Thingvalla Parsonage could speak English, and we had great difficulty in making ourselves understood; our guides, however, waited upon us as servants, and were very handy. After breakfast, we remounted and set out on our way to the Geysers, where we hoped to strike our camp that night.

Our guidebooks had led us to expect that the scenery of this ride would surpass all we had yet seen, and we certainly found it did so. Within an hour's ride of Thingvalla we reached the Hrafragja, another lava plain, though not so wide or long as the Almannagya, but which is crossed by an improvised road formed of blocks of lava. Our path led us past an extinct crater, p. 117 which, from the curious form and emissions, had long puzzled geologists: it was called a Tintron.

PONIES SWIMMING ACROSS LAKE.

This lava spout resembled the trunk of an old tree, and during an eruption the liquid flame soared through it high into the air, like water does from a hose or fire-engine. This curious volcanic spout is not the only one in the Island; further north there are several, some reaching as much as 30 feet in height. One curious thing in our 80 miles' journey to the Geysers was the number of rivers we crossed, seldom very deep, but some sufficiently so to necessitate lifting our feet from the stirrups, and laying them on the pony's back as high as possible to avoid a wetting.

One of the rivers had so many turns that we crossed and recrossed it about twenty times. The low-lying land around being all bog, it was necessary to keep our ponies to the comparatively firm shingle on the river side.

An abrupt ascent, long and steep, formed a pleasant change to the monotony of the rugged plain. Up this 'berg' our ponies wound their way zigzag between the rough boulders of rock which strewed the path. At the top we met several men with their train of ponies, waiting for us to pass them, the path being only wide enough for single file. Here we waited to give the ponies breath, and admired the view, which was wonderfully extensive. The road up looked like a ladder, so steep was it, and we wondered how the ponies could have climbed it at all. p. 118

The Icelanders are a very polite race; nearly every man you meet takes off his cap and salutes you. When meeting friends, they pull off their right hand glove and shake hands heartily. In Iceland, as elsewhere on the Continent, they also pass on the left side; indeed, I believe we English are the only nation who pass on the near side or right hand.

We halted for luncheon at a small cave, just such a place as one might expect to find Runic remains, but there were none, so we contented ourselves with eating chocolate, and letting the ponies enjoy a little grass. This cave, like many others in the Island, was used in winter as a sheep pen, the poor brutes being huddled together to prevent their being frozen to death during the long winter nights.

From here we galloped merrily on for some distance; at last we called each other's attention to an extraordinary yellow haze, like a band of London fog, across the horizon. Thicker and thicker it became: and as it rolled towards us, we realised we had encountered a regular dust-storm. Into it we rode: so thick in fact did it become, that by the time we reached the Geysers all around was hidden in yellow sand, and our eyes were filled with dust, until the tears streamed down and we were nearly blinded. It whirled round and round in its storm fury, until we were half-choked, two of our party getting very bad sore throats, produced by the irritation of the dust, as it filled eyes, nose, and mouth. It p. 119 powdered our hair also to a yellow grey, but our faces, what a sight they were! The tears had run down, making little streams amid the dust, and certainly we were hardly recognisable to one another. These dust-storms are somewhat uncommon, but proceed, in certain winds, from a large sand desert.

We pulled up at some hot springs within a few feet of the lake, which were smoking and steaming to the height of several feet, and falling down again formed numerous boiling pools. In these we put our fingers, but pulled them out quickly. Next we inserted the handles of our riding-whips: the brass bands round them turning mauve and violet from the sulphur and alum in the water; but this pretty effect soon wore off. The colour of the water and deposit round the edges of this pool were very pretty, and the bubbles as they ascended took the most lovely colours—emerald, purple, etc., turning into aqua-marine before breaking on the surface; but the odour was like terribly bad eggs. These hot springs are a curious freak of Nature, boiling and bubbling up within three feet of a cold water lake; in fact, we sat down and placed one hand in cold water and the other in hot. This was a very curious experience.

Two hours' further riding through a tract covered with willow and birch scrub, and we arrived at the 'Bruara' river. When this river is low, it can be crossed by a rudely-constructed bridge, with strong iron-clamped hand-rails on either side; but during floods it is impassable, as several feet above the p. 120 waters form a roaring cataract, when travellers have to be ferried across, at a higher point.

On we rode still through the dust-storm, over lava fields, rugged and rough in the extreme, and most weird-looking from their blackness. We passed several paths which our guide told us led into the interior of the Island, where there are still large unexplored tracts, lying at the base of a range of high snow mountains, called 'Jökull,' most of them supposed to be volcanic, but of which little is really known.

We were all getting very tired as we neared the end of our second day's ride; tired and dirty, for the sand-storm still continued. Fresh impetus was given to our ride, however, by overtaking one of the miserable party of five who had preceded us by two hours from Thingvalla. He was walking dejectedly beside his pony, too great a sufferer from inexperienced riding to remount.

Being inspired with ambition to be first in the field, we galloped past him and his companions one by one, and A. L. T. and I had the excitement of finishing our race to the Geysers. p. 121

CHAPTER X.

THE GEYSERS.

We had been told at Reykjavik it was necessary to carry tents, as there was no accommodation for travellers at the Geysers, but on arriving the wind was so strong that there was considerable difficulty in pitching them, and while our guides and gentlemen friends were making the attempt, we ladies tied up some tea in a muslin bag, and put it into a kettle, which we filled at the nearest hot spring. In a very few minutes it was infused, and with thick cream procured from the neighbouring farm, we enjoyed it much after our long dusty ride.

Just as the tent had been, as my brother thought, securely fixed, and while Vaughan and Mr Gordon were inside arranging the rugs and pack-boxes as seats, unfortunately a fresh gust of wind brought the whole affair down, burying them under the ruin. Our guides hastened to the rescue, and, more experienced in the weather forecasts than they were, advised their waiting till the wind had subsided before attempting to put up the tent again. To take our tea sitting on the pack-boxes was all we could do, encouraging each other to patience. We dare not open our boxes of eatables till the storm p. 122 had subsided, or at least until we had some shelter to protect them from a deposit of dust.

After tea we proceeded to make our inspection of the Geysers. Our first need was, however, to wash our hands and faces, so, armed with towels, sponges, and soap, we knelt at the brink of the nearest pool, and stooping down performed our ablutions, with our faces towards the east, our persons being reflected in the clear green water. We could but liken ourselves to Mahommedans, when they turn their faces towards Kibla, at Mecca, or Parsees when they kneel facing the sun, which is considered by them a representative of God.

The immediate neighbourhood of the

Geysers is not pretty; hills rise on one side, but otherwise they lie in a plain, which, when we saw it on our first arrival, was so thickly covered with sand from the storm that we could hardly discern any separate object. We hastened to examine the great Geyser. Alas! it did not, and would not play; it had done so two days previously, and we were told it was expected to renew the exploit, but, to our great mortification, it failed to do so during our visit. One of the peculiarities of this natural phenomenon is that sometimes at intervals of only a few hours it will eject columns of boiling water to the height of 100 feet, at others it will remain silent for days together. In 1770 it is recorded that this Geyser spouted eleven times in one day. Disappointed at losing the sight we had come so far to see, we turned our attention to the 'Stroker,' which is situated about p. 123 90 feet from its bigger neighbour. This also seemed in a quiescent state, but as the 'Stroker' can always be made to play by filling up the opening with earth sods, until there is no hole for the steam to escape, and it vomits the whole mass with a gigantic spout, we requested our guides to arrange for this artificial display. The emetic was consequently administered. 'Stroker' was evidently sulky, for the process had to be gone through no less than four times, whilst we waited the result in patience for at least two hours; but the display was all the better when it came.

STROKER IN ERUPTION.

I said we waited in patience, which was hardly true, as we were all on the tiptoe of excitement. Continual false alarms, and we all rushed to the 'Stroker's' side, only to be again disappointed, so we unpacked our goods, and made preparations for our evening meal, examining the Great Geyser and the hot springs meanwhile, grumbled at the smell of sulphur, and nearly despaired of the eruption ever taking place, when a sudden start from our guides, who were standing on the edge of the crater, and a shriek from them, 'He comes!' and a huge column of water ascended straight into the air for about 60 feet, the spray being ejected to a considerable distance. The eruption was accompanied by a rumbling noise and a hissing sound, as the shafts of water ascended.

We stood and watched the effect a few feet distant merely from this boiling column, feeling the rumbling distinctly under our feet and as the wind blew the steam back, it fell like rain, p. 124 quite cold, but with sufficient force to wet us uncomfortably.

This great fountain display continued in full force a quarter of an hour; then the column gradually got smaller, though steam and water issued from its mouth for a full half-hour before it quite subsided. It was a splendid spectacle, and one which left a great impression on our minds; the height of the column was fully 60 feet, and even after it had subsided, we remained some time in contemplation of its cause and effect.

Speaking of Geysers, Professor Geikie says,—

'Eruptive formations of hot water and steam, to which the general name of Geyser (*i.e.*, gusher) is given from the examples in Iceland, which were the first to be seen and described, mark a declining phase of volcanic activity. It is from irregular tube-like excrescences that the eruptions take place. The term Geyser is restricted to active openings whence columns of hot water and steam are from time to time ejected; the non-eruptive pools are only hot springs. A true Geyser should thus possess an underground pipe or passage, terminating at the surface in an opening built round with deposits of sinter. At more or less regular intervals, rumblings and sharp detonations in the pipe are followed by an agitation of water in the basin, and then the violent expulsion of a column of water and steam to a considerable height in the air.'

Dr Samuel Kneeland, in his interesting book on Iceland, says, p. 125 —

'There are two kinds of Geysers, one having jets of clear water, the other puffs of scalding vapour, coming up through a soft mud or clay of a reddish colour, probably from iron salts. In the water silica is held in solution by salts of soda, a silicate of soda being the chief ingredient. They are said to have great remediable powers; but, judging from the facility with which objects are encrusted by their silicates, it would seem as if their free use would soon turn a person to stone. The geyserite, or the solid incrustations, is over 80° of silica, with 3° alumina, and a little magnesia, iron, potash, and soda.'

One thing I looked for in vain at these Geysers, namely, the pretty-coloured mud which is found at the Yellowstone Park of America, and which I had often heard my father and brother describe. In New Zealand the Geyser mud was formerly used by the Maoris as a kind of porridge, which they were very fond of. It is a pity the starving Icelanders cannot do likewise.

I wish our party could have been photographed as it stood round the 'Stroker,' waiting for the display, everybody's face a picture of expectation, which changed to disappointment at the long time we had to wait. As 'little things please little minds,' to pass the time, Miss T. and I were trundled about in the wheelbarrow in which the old men had brought the sods for the Geyser's emetic from the farm; an occasional upset made our ride all the more amusing. It was a ride p. 126 worth noting, as it was performed in one of the very few wheeled conveyances in the Island.

By the time the exhibition of the Geyser was over, the wind had lulled, the sandstorm had ceased, and our tents had been successfully pitched. In the larger tent we dined, and for such an out-of-the-way place, it was so wonderful a meal that I must describe it. We were sitting on the pack-boxes inside the tent, waited on by two guides. First there was ox-tail soup quite hot, the tin having been placed in a neighbouring hot spring—the Blissa—for twenty minutes. We had no soup plates, but tumblers served the occasion, being afterwards washed by the guides, and made ready for further use.

Tinned meat-collops followed, splendidly hot, and to us hungry mortals appeared excellent. The third course was tongue, followed by tinned apricots and thick cream. Alas! we had no spoons, and how to eat our cream and apricots was a puzzle. Our guide, whom we had christened 'Johnny,' to his great delight, helped us out of this difficulty. He produced some horn spoons which he had carved during the long winter evenings, and which he offered to sell to us for a krone a-piece. It was quite high price enough, notwithstanding the carving, but the necessity of the occasion made us glad to close with his offer. Cheese, biscuit, and figs concluded our magnificent repast.

After dinner, another inspection of the great p. 127 Geyser, to see if it was more inclined to favour us with a display of its power, but a fruitless one; a walk amongst the hot springs, and then, as it was bitterly cold, we decided to turn in for the night. Our tents were pitched exactly half way between the great Geyser and the 'Stroker.' The large tent was to serve for the three gentlemen and the two guides, and the smaller one for Miss T. and myself.

We had secured some bundles of hay for our beds, and our mackintosh sheets were used to cover over them. My brother undertook to make our beds, and arrange our tent for the night, and disappeared inside, carrying with him the rugs, air-pillows, etc., necessary for the purpose.

On his returning and telling us all was ready, Miss T. and myself bid the party good-night. We had not till then realised the height of our bedchamber, and how to enter it was a puzzle. It was not like the big tent, which would hold a dozen people standing erect, but a tiny gipsy tent, the opening so low, we literally had to crawl in on our hands and knees, whilst the whole community stood round watching us, and laughing heartily.

Once inside, our difficulties were not over, for we found the sides of the tent so low that we could only sit up straight in the middle. So we could do no more than partially undress and roll ourselves in our fur cloaks and rugs. With the exception of waking now and then to listen to the p. 128 rumblings we had been told to expect before the eruption of the Great Geyser, we spent a tolerably comfortable night, notwithstanding we were surrounded by boiling, seething waters on every side, and were in hopeful expectation of the big Geyser's eruption. By the morning we had got quite accustomed to the sulphurous odours.

We had several visitors in the early morning, who thrust under our tent such articles as jewellery, saddle-cloths, carved spoons, etc., for sale. We bargained for some of these, and ultimately obtained them. The prices at first asked were absurdly high, but these simple-minded Icelanders have an idea that our nation's liberality is unbounded.

There is really little good old jewellery left in the Island, in consequence of the extreme poverty of the natives, who have sold to travellers the greater portion of that which they possessed.

How to dress in our three feet tent, was a problem which for some time our minds failed to solve, and still more, how and where to wash, until the gentlemen informed us that as they were going to the springs to bathe, their tent was at our disposal for as long as we wished. Here we found that their forethought had provided a large tub from the farm, which they had filled with warm water, so, after all, we had a luxurious bath.

When our only looking-glass was passed round, we each in turn exclaimed, 'How fearfully burnt I p. 129 am!' and so indeed we were. Our yachting caps and deerstalkers had been shade enough on board ship, but not for a four days' ride across country in wind and a dust storm.

We had arrived at our journey's end, had seen the 'Stroker' at any rate play, and now if we wished to catch our steamer at Reykjavik, we had no time to lose in preparing for our return journey, so after breakfast, while our guides collected our steeds, packed the tents, etc., we started for a final look at the Geysers and the hot springs, which so abound in this neighbourhood. There are, I believe, no less than fifty within the circuit of half a mile. These springs lie at the base of a mountain of no great height, the tract in which these thermal waters is found being about 700 yards in length and 300 in width.

The Great Geyser lies to the north of this plain, its basin, 60 feet in diameter, is at the summit of a mound 20 feet in height, composed of silica, a mineral that the Geyser water holds in solution, and which from the constant overflowing of the water, deposits layers of beautiful enamel, which at the top is too hard to detach, although round the base soft and crumbly. The basin is nearly circular, and is generally, except after an eruption, full to the brim, and always steaming, the water at the bottom being about 228° Fahr.

The tube in the centre, from which the water spouts is about 10 feet across, and I read somewhere that on measuring down about 70 feet, p. 130 the tube took a sudden turn which prevented further soundings. The water is ejected at a heat of 180° or 190° Fahr., and rises over 100 feet into the air.

These Geysers are nearly 400 feet above sea level.

The formation of the 'Stroker' differs from that of the Great Geyser in not having any basin round its well, the latter being in shape like a rough test-tube, about 8 feet in diameter and 36 feet deep, with two pipe-mouths. After the eruption witnessed by 'Burton,' he noticed that 'the level of the water in the tube was at a depth of 25 feet, where might be seen, partly submerged, the mouths of two pipes entering at different angles, close together on the side nearest the Great Geyser. From these pipes steam belched forth at intervals with considerable force, churning the water in the well round rapidly.'

It is strange that the eruptions of the 'Stroker' do not affect the water in the well of the Great Geyser, though it is not 100 yards off, while on the other hand, when the Geyser is in eruption, the water of the 'Stroker' subsides.

It really was very tantalising to have come so far, and be within a few hours' distance of Hecla, and yet have to return without having visited it. Besides, from what we gathered, we could well have exhausted another week in expeditions in the neighbourhood, but snow-capped Hecla, the ice-clad heights of the Jöklar, and the Red Crater, with innumerable other interesting excursions of Icelandic note, had to be left for a future visit, if ever we should make it, to the Island.

The name of Hecla means a mantle: its last eruption occurred in 1845. Where is Hecla? Who has not been asked that question at school? and little did I think, when learning geography, that I should ever see it, even at a distance. Alas! time would not allow us a nearer acquaintance. Visiting it meant either seventeen days round the Island in a Danish boat, or waiting six weeks for the *Camoens*, circumstances over which we had no control made both impossible, and we had reluctantly to give up the excursion. While these volcanoes and their adjuncts must ever remain, from their uncertain eruptions, a cause of terror to the inhabitants—boiling and bubbling for years, and then suddenly bursting forth, to the entire destruction of all around—they have, we know also, a beneficial effect in the world's domestic economy. What, for instance, would happen to Britain were it not for the Gulf Stream? It would be as cold as Labrador. The streams in the Gulf of Mexico are fed from equatorial currents and boiling springs, and rush on to the North Atlantic 25° or 30° warmer than the sea through which it passes, warming the air of Western Europe.

Again, hot springs (caused by subterranean fires), which, from their curative celebrity, attract visitors and invalids, mean business, and business means money to the inhabitants of the locality.

Taking our last farewell of these seething pools, which bubbled and boiled around us, I could not help wondering what kind of commotion could be going on beneath the earth's surface. A power that could thus eject 100 feet of boiling water into the air, and not burst asunder the surrounding ground, was indeed a marvellous phenomenon. The Iceland Geysers, which were the first discovered, as well as those of New Zealand (so soon to be destroyed), and those of the Yellowstone Park, must ever be of enormous interest to the traveller and geologist, and with regret we turned our backs upon them, having reached the turning-point of our journey and the limit of our time. Time waits on no man, so we tore ourselves away, feeling, however, we had seen in the Iceland Geysers one of the greatest marvels of Nature.

Various explanations of Geysers have been attempted by scientific men, and as some of my readers may take sufficient interest in these wonderful phenomena to wish to know something regarding the causes which originate them, I have got my father to write a short chapter on what he saw and thought of the great Geysers in the volcanic district of the Yellowstone Park, which I have appended at the end of my narrative.

Drinking Horn or Powder Flask. Two-thumbed Glove. Twisted Sheeps Horns. Straps for tying on packs. Icelandic Whip, leather thong. Snuff box. Horn Spoon. Skin Shoes. *Etched F.P.F. from sketch by Author.*
p. 133

CHAPTER XI.

FARM HOUSE.

We traversed nearly the same road on our return journey from the Geysers as we had taken *en route*, our first halt being made at the farm near which we had lunched the previous day, situated close to the winding river we had crossed so often. In our up journey, we had had no time to spare, so could not visit the farm

house and buildings. Indeed the Icelanders are very chary of exhibiting their domestic arrangements and dwellings, hence it is difficult at all times to visit their homes. However, I was determined to see over a farm house before leaving the Island, so wandered around until we found an old woman. By shaking hands with her, and praising up her skyr, we made her understand by signs that we wished to see the house and byre. These were built of peat and rubble, with grass roofs, on one of which a cow was actually grazing at the time. Outside, drying in the sun, were pieces of peat in size about two feet by three, and about two inches thick; they were doubled, tent-fashion, to enable the air to pass through, and were standing in a row along a turf wall. On inquiring their use, we learnt they were intended as a species of saddle-cloth for the pack ponies, to protect the vertebrae. The peat being placed on the animal's back, the loads are attached on either side by a rope made of the mane and tail hair of the ponies, plaited neatly in three, either black and white or brown and white, and mixed with a little flax, they really form quite a pretty adornment to the trappings; the loops through which the ropes pass are of carved sheep's horns, knotted into most fantastic shapes.

We first visited the dairy, composed of peat and rubble as usual. Inside, placed on a shelf, were large basins of milk and cream, as in England. Sheep and cows' milk were side by side, for this farmer was a wealthy man, and the happy possessor of a few cattle. He had butter too, waiting to be sent to Reykjavik, which we tasted and found very good, and an old-fashioned churn, some three feet high, like a chimney-pot with a rod down the middle, terminating in a piece of flat wood. Of this churn the old lady seemed very proud, and she was quite delighted when I lifted the rod up and down, to find I knew how to use it. I believe that won her heart.

Leaving the dairy, the old woman took my hand and dragged me along a perfectly dark passage, Miss T. following. This passage was paved with stones, and had stone walls on either side. Half stifled with peat smoke, we arrived, puffing and panting, in the kitchen. Here in a corner was the p. 135 big peat fire which filled the whole dwelling with its exhalations. All around was perfect blackness, until our eyes got accustomed to the dim hazy light, when we espied a woman in a corner making cakes, formed of two layers of meal buttered and placed at the bottom of a huge cauldron, such as is used by the Irish peasantry for boiling potatoes. These cakes served hot are very palatable.

There was no chimney; the smoke merely escaped the best way it could through a small hole, around which some hams were being smoked. They must have been mutton hams, for there are no pigs from which to get others; and mutton hams properly smoked are very good too.

We were next conducted through another long dark passage, down which we stumbled, bumping our heads against the side walls, there being no entrance of light whatever, save what came through the doorway from the reflection of the embers of the peat fire. So dark was the passage, we almost fancied we were going through a coal mine. After a time we reached a second room, devoted to the storing of packets of dried fish and huge barrels of skyr; but the want of ventilation and light in this quaint Icelandic larder was sadly felt.

Where did the family sleep? we asked ourselves, after visiting another such apartment. Finally, by sundry gesticulations, we succeeded in making our old friend understand our question, when off she led us to the family bedroom. Imagine a long passage room with a small window at either end, p. 136 containing seven wooden beds, placed so that five joined head and foot along one wall, while the other two were on either side of the door. Here the whole family disposed of themselves at night.

In one of the beds lay a poor sick child. From her wasted appearance one might suppose she was in a consumption, but this fatal disease is unknown in Iceland.

In another bed lay a poor old woman, who as I addressed her grinned at me so horribly, in the dim-light, that she had the appearance of an awful old witch, and afforded a great contrast to the fragile child in the adjoining bed. Each bed was covered by an old-fashioned patch-work quilt.

Stowed away among the low rafters of the roof I noticed a spinning-wheel and paraffin lamp, and some clothes packed in little tight bundles; much as I should have liked to stop and take in a few more details, my nasal organs could stand no more, and, feeling somewhat faint, I had, *nolens volens*, to make a rush for the door. Much to my regret, I did not dare venture inside again to further inspect this curious bedchamber.

Our old lady bade us a most affectionate farewell, returning several times to shake us warmly by the hand, but distinctly refusing our proffered krone.

About half way between the Geysers and Thingvalla we recrossed the famous Bruara Fall. From bank to bank it is probably 200 feet, but in fine weather a crossing can be made by a little bridge which spans some 6 feet of babbling, seething water p. 137 at the narrowest part of the rocks, where the river forms two cascades. The bridge is old and rickety, and as the water is of considerable depth and tremendous volume, the bridge is hardly a desirable halting-place for any length of time, although the view from its planks is very fascinating.

We passed that night once more in the parsonage at Thingvalla, but much more comfortably than before, as we had engaged all the rooms beforehand, and also ordered a good fish dinner to be ready for us on our arrival.

As to meat, we did not expect to get it; beef is hardly ever eaten by the Icelanders, being too expensive to procure. The native sheep are usually killed towards the end of September, and the meat salted or smoked for winter consumption. Formerly horse-flesh was much eaten in the Island, but is not so now. This struck us as strange in a place where such a scarcity of food exists, and where ponies abound. Having tasted it myself while in Germany, I know it is by no means to be despised.

The principal vegetables to be had in Iceland are turnips and potatoes, and of these there is only a limited supply; so that really fish remains the one staple diet of the Island,—on the coast this is eaten fresh, but it is dried before being packed and sent into the interior—cod, salmon, haddock, trout, halibut, herrings, flounders, and sometimes sharks.

The next morning, as soon as we had break p. 138 fasted, we mounted our ponies with the regretful feeling the day's ride would be our last in Iceland. We had been unfortunate in missing the clergyman at Thingvalla both going and returning: we regretted it the more as we heard that he was a very clever man and a good English scholar. Our good-natured hostess, however, had done her best to supply his place, and we bade her a hearty farewell, with much shaking of hands. Off we went at a gallop, traversing the same route, fording the same rivers as on our up journey, arriving safely at Reykjavik on the fourth day from that on which we had left it, having compassed the 160 miles in three and a half days with comparatively little fatigue, which I attribute to our mode of riding being so much easier a movement than sitting sideways with a half twisted body. I can only repeat what I before said, that we should never have accomplished this long and fatiguing ride so easily, and in such a short time, either in a chair or on a side saddle; so if any lady should follow our example, and go to Iceland, let her be prepared to defy Mrs Grundy, and ride as a man.

We had certainly every reason to be contented with the result of our trip to the Geysers. The weather had been favourable,—very hot sometimes in the middle of the day, but cold at night; but this was rather refreshing than otherwise, and the scenery had well repaid our toil and trouble. The Icelandic landscapes do not lack colour, as has been asserted by some travellers; whilst the clearness p. 139 of the atmosphere is wonderful, and the shades of blue, purple, carmine, and yellow in the sky melting into one another produce most lovely effects.

Unquestionably the landscape lacks trees and verdure, and one missed the gorgeous autumn colouring of our English woods, for there is no foliage, only low scrub jungle. It seems very doubtful if Iceland was ever wooded, as is supposed by some persons, as no trees of any size have as yet been discovered in the peat beds, a very conclusive evidence to the contrary.

Iceland is so sparsely populated that one often rides miles without encountering a human being. Even in the little town of Sauderkrok there is not much life in the streets; for instance, A. L. T. dropped his pipe as we rode out of the town, and on our return, eight hours later, we found it in the centre of a small street, exactly where he had dropped it. Now, as a pipe is a coveted luxury to an Icelander, it is presumable that no one could have passed along that street in our absence.

It was just 3 p.m. when we entered Reykjavik, having accomplished our last day's ride from Thingvalla in six and a half hours. The *Camoens* was still safely at anchor in the harbour, and we rejoiced at having returned without a single *contretemps*.

On our way through Reykjavik to the ship Mr Gordon ordered dinner at the hotel to be ready by 7 o'clock, and we looked forward to this repast p. 140 with much pleasure after our tinned meat and biscuit diet of the last few days.

Before returning on board to change our riding dresses, we went in search of the washing. In a queer little wooden house, at the back of the town, we found the washerman, who smiled and nodded, and asked 3s. for what would have cost 30s. in England, handing us an enormous linen bag, in which the things were packed. This was consigned to A. L. T., who carried it in both arms through the town, and ultimately on board, where it landed quite dry; and to our surprise we found our linen had been most beautifully washed and got up, quite worthy of a first-class laundry.

The dinner was excellent, everything being very hot, and served in Danish style. As is the universal custom among the better class, the hostess waited on us herself, and told us she had spun her own dress and the sitting-room carpet the winter before, and always wove her own linen. This was our last evening ashore, as we were to heave anchor at midnight on Tuesday, 17th August, and in four and a half days we were, if all went well, to find ourselves back in Scotland. Alas! these expectations were not realised, as few human aspirations are!

During our four days' absence to the Geysers, the captain and crew had been engaged in shipping no less than 617 ponies, which additional cargo caused two days' delay. Poor little beasts, when we arrived on board we found they had all been so tightly stowed away as not to be able to lie down. p. 141 Fine sturdy little animals they appeared, mostly under seven years of age, and in excellent condition; a very different sight to what they were on arriving at Granton, when, after six and a half days' voyage, every rib showed distinctly through their wasted, tucked up forms.

After our dinner we lounged about in Reykjavik, paying a farewell visit to the few objects of interest it has for travellers, most of which have already been cursorily noticed in a previous chapter.

We spent some little time in the Museum again, which, after all, is not much of an exhibition, for, as our cicerone, the hotel-keeper's daughter, Fräulein Johannison, explained, all the best curiosities had been carried off to Denmark. I naturally looked everywhere in the little Museum for an egg of the Great Auk, or a stuffed specimen of the bird, but there was neither, which struck me as rather curious, considering Iceland was originally the home of this now extinct species. Not even an egg has been found for over forty years, although diligent search has been made by several well-known naturalists. The Great Auk was never a pretty bird; it was large in size, often weighing 11 lb. It had a duck's bill, and small eyes, with a large unwieldy body, and web feet. Its wings were extremely small and ugly, from long want of use, so the bird's movements on land were slow, and it was quite incapable of flight. On the water it swam fast and well.

There are only about ten complete specimens of p. 142 this bird, and about seventy eggs, known to exist In March 1888, one of these eggs was sold by auction for £225.

From the Museum we entered some of the stores, and purchased a fair collection of photographs, some skin shoes, snuff-boxes, buckles, and other native curios; we than returned to the hotel, paid our bill, bade our host, hostess, and guides farewell, with many regretful shakes of the hand on either side, and finally quitted Icelandic ground about 9 p.m.

The evening was lovely, and after arranging our cabins we remained some time on deck watching the Northern Lights, which illuminated the entire heavens, and were most beautiful. Unfortunately we did not see the 'Aurora Borealis,' which in these latitudes is often visible.

The following afternoon as we were passing the curious rocky Westmann Islands, we slacked steam, to allow an old man in a boat to get the mail bag thrown over to him. He had rowed out some three miles to fetch the mail, and the bag contained exactly one letter, and a few newspapers. Steaming on again we sighted no more land until Scotland came in view, which we reached on Sunday afternoon. What a passage we had! It was rough going to Iceland, but nothing to be compared to our return voyage! We sat on deck, either with our chairs lashed, or else holding on to ropes until our hands were quite benumbed with cold, while huge waves, at least 15 feet high, dashed over the p. 143 ship, often over the bridge itself. If we opened our cabin portholes for a little fresh air, which at times was really a necessity, the cabin was soon flooded, and our clothes and rugs spent half their time being dried in the donkey engine room.

Eleven of the poor ponies died, and had to be thrown overboard, a serious loss to their owners; but one could not help wondering that more of them did not succumb, so closely were they packed together, with very little air but that afforded by the windsails. It was marvellous how the sailors managed to drag out the dead from the living mass of animals. This they accomplished by walking on the backs of the survivors, and roping the dead animals, drew the carcases to the centre hold of the ship, when the crane soon brought them to the surface, and consigned them to a watery grave.

For six days the live cargo of beasts had to balance themselves with the ship's movement in these turbulent seas without one moment's respite or change of position. No wonder that on arriving at Granton they were in a miserable plight. Within five minutes, however, of our being roped to the pier they were being taken off in horse boxes, three at a time, and the entire number were landed in three hours.

The hot air from the stables was at times overpowering, notwithstanding that eight windsails were kept over it, which as they flapped in the wind, looked just like eight ghosts. p. 144

The *Camoens* was a steady sea boat, but better adapted for cargo than for passengers, especially lady passengers, and the captain did not disguise that he preferred not having the latter on board. Once in calm water we discovered we had seriously shifted our cargo, and lay all over on one side, so much so that a cup of tea could not stand, the slant being great, although the water was perfectly calm.

Well, we had accomplished our trip, and very much we had enjoyed it. We had really seen Iceland, that far off region of ice and snow, and had returned safely. The six days on board ship passed pleasantly enough for us; we had got accustomed to roughing it, and were all very good friends with each other, and the few other passengers. We found one of these especially interesting; he was a scientific Frenchman, who had been sent to Iceland to write a book for the Government, and being a very poor English scholar was very glad to find some one who could converse in his native tongue. We hardly saw a ship the whole way, but we saw plenty of whales, not, however, the kind which go to Dundee, where the whalebone fetches from £1200 to £2000 a ton.

We brought an enormous skeleton home which was found off the coast of Iceland; and such an immense size; it was sent to England as a curiosity for some museum.

Occasionally we had lovely phosphorescent effects, and as we neared Scotland, millions of p. 145 pink and brown jelly-fish filled the water. At Thurso we hailed a boat to send telegrams ashore—such a collection!—to let our various friends know we had returned in safety from Ultima Thule. That night as we passed Aberdeen we entered calm water, and there was hardly a ripple all the way to Granton, where we landed at 3.30 on Monday, 23d August, exactly twenty-four days from starting.

Such a lovely day! The Forth looked perfect as we steamed up to our harbour anchorage. The grand hills and rocks and the fine old Castle were a contrast to poor little Reykjavik, the capital of Iceland. The pretty town, and the trees, how we enjoyed the sight of the latter, for we had seen no trees for weeks, and their green looked most pleasing amongst the stone buildings.

How busy, how civilised everything appeared! When will trains and carts traverse the Northern Isle we had just left? Oh, but where are the emigrants? Let us go and watch their surprised faces as they catch the first glimpse of this new scene. We went, and were sorely disappointed. They were merely standing together with their backs to the view, putting on their boots, or occupied about minor matters, taking no notice whatever of their surroundings, and receiving no new impressions. It must require a civilised mind, we suppose, to appreciate civilisation, just as it requires talent to appreciate talent. p. 146

Below is a table of our expenditure during our trip, which may perhaps prove of service to one wishing to enjoy an uncommon autumn holiday:—

Five people travelling together for twenty-five days disbursed each £20, 1s. 8d.

Passage Money round Island and return,	£8	3	0
Food, 6s. 6d. a day,	6	3	0
Steward, 10s.	0	10	0
Food taken from London, £2, 10s., or 10s. each,	0	10	0
Four days' ride to Geysers; two nights Thingvalla; ponies, guides, tents, sods, pasturage for ponies; milk, coffee, etc.,	4	0	0
Akureyri; going ashore, dinner, pony, etc.,	0	6	10
Sauderkrok; " skyr, coffee, etc.,	0	6	0
Bordeyri; " " " "	0	5	10
	£20	1	8

Wine not included.

Purchases, photos, washing, stamps, and other individual personal expenses extra.

p. 147

CHAPTER XII.

VOLCANOES.

In the foregoing pages it may seem strange that hardly any allusion has been made to the special characteristic of Iceland, viz., its volcanic structure, or to the numerous lava floods which, bursting forth in furious molten streams, have from time to time devastated its surface, leaving in their track a chaos of disrupted rocks, chasms, vast fissures, and subterranean caverns.

Our trip to Iceland was, however, unfortunately so limited in duration as to preclude, save in our four days' ride to the Great Geyser tract, any extension of travel in the various volcanic regions. Hence the omission. I have therefore extracted the following data relative to its principal volcanoes and their eruptions from such books of reference [a] as have been available to me.

The annexed compilation will, I think, explain to such of my readers as are not acquainted with the geological strata of Iceland, its sterile nature, the extreme poverty of its inhabitants, and the constant terror under which their existence is p. 148 passed, lest a fresh outbreak of lava should sweep away both them and their homesteads. It is somewhat singular, that although Iceland may be looked upon as a veritable mass of volcanoes and hot springs—for with the exception of some 4000 square miles of habitable ground, it may be said literally to rest on underground fires, and while the various eruptions of Etna, Vesuvius, and other volcanoes have for centuries been watched and recorded in the public papers with interest—it is only comparatively recently that the awe-inspiring volcanic eruptions of Iceland have been brought into notice. For instance, while full fifty pages in Ree's 'Cyclopædia' are devoted to the subject of volcanoes, those of Iceland are barely touched upon; yet their eruptions are by far the most devastating on record. So limited, indeed, formerly were the researches of science in these ice-clad regions, that for long Hecla was quoted as its only volcano.

[a] Mrs Somerville's 'Physical Geography;' Chambers' 'Encyclopædia;' Ree's 'Cyclopædia;' Lyell's 'Geology;' Mr George Lock's 'Guide to Iceland.'

Now that the Island has attracted the further notice of geologists, it has been shown that there exist no less than twenty volcanic mountains, all of which have been in active eruption within historic times, and nearly one hundred eruptions have been chronicled as having taken place in the Island.

Although Hecla is doubtless the best known of the Iceland volcanoes, it is by no means the largest; that of 'Askja' (a basket), far surpasses it in size. This latter volcano lies in a great central desert termed 'Odaxa-hraun' or 'Misdeed Lava Desert,' covering a space of 1200 square miles, and p. 149 a most appropriate name it is, for the devastation caused by its last flood of lava is indescribable.

In one of the convulsions of this mountain in 1875, a quantity of lava five miles in circumference was disrupted, sinking into the mountain to a depth of 710 feet, and causing an earthquake which was felt all over the island. In one region, viz., that of the 'Myvatn's Orœfi' or 'Midge Lake Desert,' a fissure was opened which extended over 20 miles in a north-easterly direction, through which molten lava flowed continuously for four months after the earthquake. Although this fissure is at least 30 miles from Askja, so great was the column of fire thrown up by the eruption, that it was visible for four successive days at Reykjavik, 100 miles distant. The study of an Icelandic map will show the numerous volcanic ranges of mountains which intersect the island in almost every direction.

To the north there will be seen a wonderful volcanic tract. So vast, in fact, that Professor Johnstrup has termed it the Fire Focus of the North. To the north-east, again, is found a large lake, called 'Myvata,' or 'Midge Lake,' with a volcanic range of mountains which stretch from north to south; the most famous of these are 'Leivhnukr,' and 'Krafla,' which, after years of quiescence, poured forth such an amount of lava into the adjoining lake that for many days its waters stood at boiling heat. Other volcanoes in this region eject with terrible force a quantity of boiling mineral pitch, throwing up the dark matter completely p. 150 enveloped in steam, accompanied by horrible rumbling noises.

Sir George Mackenzie, in his travels in Iceland, thus describes one of the deposits:—

'It is impossible,' he says, 'to convey any idea of the wonders of its terrors, or the sensations of a person even of strong nerves standing on a support which but feebly bears him, and below which fire and brimstone are in incessant action, having before his eyes tremendous proof of what is going on beneath him; enveloped in thick vapour, his ears stunned with thundering noises—such a situation can only be conceived by one who has experienced it.'

The extent of the sulphur beds too in this region are beyond calculation: they reproduce themselves every few years. In the vicinity of 'Krafla' is a curious rock, composed of obsidian, a substance which closely resembles black glass.

To the south of the Island is another volcano, termed the 'Kotlugja,' or 'Cauldron Rift,' lying among glaciers known as the 'Myrdals Jökull,' whose eruptions, thirteen of which have been noted, are considered to have done more mischief than any others in the Island. Between the Myrdals and the 'Orœja Jökla' lies one of the most noted volcanoes of Iceland—the 'Skaptar-Jökull,' whose eruption in 1783 is chronicled in all works on Iceland, as the prodigious floods of lava it poured forth in that year were unparalleled in historic times. The molten streams rushing seaward, down the rivers and valleys, the glowing p. 151 lava leaping over precipices and rocks, which in after years, when they have cooled down, resemble petrified cataracts, and now form one of the grand scenic attractions of the Island.

In Mrs Somerville's 'Physical Geography,' she vividly describes this eruption, narrating how, commencing in May 1783, it continued pouring forth its fiery streams with unabated fury until the following August. So great was the amount of vapour, that the sun was hidden for months, whilst clouds of ashes were carried hundreds of miles out to sea. The quantity of matter ejected on this occasion was calculated at from fifty to sixty thousand millions of cubic yards. The burning lava flowed in a stream in some places 20 to 30 miles broad, filling up the beds of rivers, and entering the sea at a distance of 50 miles from where the eruption occurred. Some of the rivers were not only heated to boiling point, but were dried up, and the condensed vapour fell as snow and rain. Epidemic disease followed in the wake of this fearful lava flood. It was calculated that no less than 1300 persons, and 150,000 sheep and cattle perished, 20 villages were destroyed. The eruption lasted two years.

Mr Paulson, a geologist, who visited Iceland eleven years later, found smoke still issuing from the rocks in the locality.

The heat of this eruption not only re-melted old lavas, and opened fresh subterranean caverns, but one of its streams was computed to course the plains to an extent of 50 miles, with a depth of 100 feet, p. 152 and 12 to 15 feet broad. Another stream was calculated at 40 miles long, and 7 wide. Men, their cattle and homesteads, their churches and grazing lands, were burnt up, whilst noxious vapours not only filled the air, but even shrouded the light of the sun.

The terrible convulsions which occurred in Iceland during the year 1783, were greater than those recorded at any other period. About a month previously to the convulsion of 'Skaptar-Jökull,' a submarine volcano burst out at sea, and so much pumice stone was ejected that the sea was covered with it for 150 miles round, ships being stopped in their course, whilst a new island was thrown up, which the King of Denmark claimed, and named Nyöe, or New Island. Before the year had elapsed, however, it as speedily disappeared, leaving only a reef of rocks some 30 fathoms under water to mark its site.

But what of Hecla? which is 5000 feet high, and is situated close to the coast at the Southern end of a low valley, lying between two vast parallel table lands covered with ice.

If the eruptions of Hecla are not considered to have been quite so devastating as those just recorded of the 'Skap-tar-Jökull,' their duration has been longer, some of them having lasted six years at a time.

When Sir George Mackenzie visited Hecla, he found its principal crater 100 feet deep, and curiously enough, it contained a quantity of snow at the bottom. There are many smaller craters near its summit, the surrounding rocks, consisting chiefly p. 153 of lava and basalt, are covered with loose stones, scoria, and ashes.

A record of the eruptions of Hecla has been chronicled since the 10th century, and they number 43. One of its most violent convulsions occurred in the same year as that of the 'Skaptar-Jökull,' viz., in 1783. At a distance of two miles from the crater, the lava flood was one mile wide, and 40 feet deep, whilst its fine dust was scattered as far as the Orkney Islands, 400 miles distant.

The mountain itself is composed of sand, grit, and ashes, several kinds of pumice stone being thrown out of it. It also ejects a quantity of a species of black jaspars, which look as if they had been burned at the extremities, while in form they resemble trees and branches. All the different kinds of lava found in volcanoes are to be met with here, such as agate, pumice stone, and both black and green lapis obsidian. These lavas are not all found near the place of eruption, but at some distance, and on their becoming cold form arches and caverns, the crust of which being hard rock. The smaller of the caverns are now used by the Icelanders for sheltering their cattle. The largest of the caves known is 5034 feet long and from 50 to 54 feet broad and from 34 to 36 feet high.

It is believed by some geologists that a subterranean channel connects the volcanic vent of Hecla with the great central one of Askja. This theory is based on the fact that a number of lava floods have burst forth simultaneously at different times p. 154 at great distances from the volcanoes, leading to the supposition that innumerable subterranean channels exist in the neighbourhood.

The eruptions attributed to the volcano of Hecla vary much in number, some authorities saying there have been 40. Mrs Somerville quotes them at 23, and Mr Locke, in his 'Guide to Iceland,' at 17 in number. In the latter's work is given a table of most of its principal eruptions. One of these was of a singular nature; huge chasms opened in the earth, and for three days the wells and fountains became as white as milk, and new hot springs sprang into existence.

The twelfth eruption of this mountain was also of unusual violence. It occurred in January 1597. For twelve days previously to the outbreak loud reports were heard all over the Island, while no less than eighteen columns of fire were seen ascending from it during its eruption. The ashes it threw out covered half the Island.

The seventeenth eruption commenced on the 2d September 1845, and continued for seven months. On this occasion the ashes were carried over to Shetland, and the columns of smoke rising from the mountain reached a height of 14,000 Danish feet.

Such is a brief description of the tremendous forces which dominate Iceland. Here Nature works in silence for long periods beneath the crust of the earth, and then, with little or no forewarning, bursts forth in uncontrollable fury, ruthlessly devastating with its fiery streams whatever impedes its course. p. 155

Who can wonder that, under such existing terrors, the scanty inhabitants of the Island are a sad and dejected race. A people with death and terror continually at their doors can hardly be otherwise; whilst competitive industry, energy, and hopeful prosperity are alike suppressed by the constant devastations which occur.

With respect to the Thermal Springs, these must be considered as products of the same underground fires, and which form a second characteristic of Iceland.

These Springs may be divided into three kinds, viz., those of unceasing ebullition, those which are only sometimes eruptive, and wells which merely contain tepid water, though supposed to have been formerly eruptive.

Professor Bunsen, who passed eleven

days by the side of the Great Geyser in Iceland, attributes the phenomenon to the molecular changes which take place in water after being subjected to heat. In such circumstances, water loses much of the air condensed in it, and the cohesion of the molecules is thereby increased, and a higher temperature required to boil it. In this state, when boiled, the production of vapour is so instantaneous as to cause an explosion.

Professor Bunsen found that the water at the bottom of the great Icelandic Geyser had a higher temperature than that of boiling water, and that this temperature increasing, finally caused its eruption.

In America, among the hot springs warmed by subterranean vapours, such as those springing from p. 156 the sides of 'Nuerode Chilian,' the hot springs gush out through a bed of perpetual snow.

Among the hot springs of Iceland, Mr G. Loch gives an interesting description of those known as the 'Northern Geyser' and its tributary springs. One of these, the 'Uxhaver' or 'Ox Spring' is named from an Ox having fallen into it, and in a short time having been thrown out in the form of boiled beef. This hot spring emanates from an oval basin, 30 feet in circumference, and 4 feet in diameter. Its spurts are very regular, occurring about every 6 minutes, and about 10 feet high. After a spurt the water in the basin is lowered from 4 to 6 feet, but quickly refills, whilst the water thrown up is clear as crystal, and its spray glistening in the sun's rays has a most beautiful effect.

The smaller springs in this so-called 'Uxhaver' group are collected in a bed of rock 280 feet from the principal Geyser, and it is singular that although separated from it by only 300 yards of boggy ground, the springs in each bed of rock seem to have a distinct source of supply, for they are not affected by each other's spoutings. It is impossible even to enumerate the various hot springs of Iceland, as they are spread over all its volcanic region.

I must here bring my little book to a close, and if it has done no more than make my readers desire to make a personal acquaintance with this wonderful little Island, so full of natural curiosities, so abounding in ancient history, so isolated, and so quaint, it will have served its object.

p. 157

APPENDIX.

WHAT IS A GEYSER?

Having been requested by my daughter to add to her little book a short explanatory chapter on the marvellous phenomenon of Nature she saw in Iceland, commonly called a Geyser, I herewith subjoin the results of a few of the observations and reflections I made while visiting the great geysers of the volcanic districts of Wyoming and Montana, in the autumn of 1884.

In order to make the matter perfectly clear, let me say at the very outset that a geyser is simply a volcano from which a quantity of superheated boiling water, saturated with mineral matter, is paroxysmally ejected high into the air. Instead of, as in the case of fire volcanoes, the ejected matters being smoke, flame, lava, scoria, pumice stone, and scalding mud. Moreover, while the eruptions from all volcanoes are intermittent—that is to say, every kind of volcano has alternating periods of activity and repose—the eruptions from p. 158 geysers further differ from the fire and flame ejections of burning mountains, with their other attendant phenomena, in occurring at definite periods of time, and being of equally definite durations. It is this life-like periodicity in the geyser's mode of action which makes it as awe-inspiring to behold as it is puzzling to explain.

That hot water should issue in a continuous and but little varying sized stream from the bowels of the earth, with a force sufficient to carry it high into the air, has nothing whatever wonderful about it. Such a natural phenomenon may be witnessed at many places. For example, it may be seen doing so everyday at the white foaming, frothing, natural mineral water sprudel of Nauheim, or at any artificially bored artesian well, such as the celebrated one at Paris. Nor does the mere intermittence of water issuing from the bowels of the earth suffice to surprise one. For such natural phenomena are seen at Bolder-Born, in Westphalia; the Lay-Well, at Torbay; the Giggleswick Well, in Yorkshire; and even on a small scale at St Anthony's Well, Arthur's Seat, Edinburgh; all which occurrences are readily explicable on ordinary hydraulic principles, and quite different things from geyser action, which try to explain it as you will, always runs into a volcanic groove. Yet the periodicity of a geyser's action cannot be said to be entirely due to volcanic agency. For the mere action of heat on the solids of the earth's crust, or even of heat in simple conjunction with water, according to either p. 159 Mackenzie or Tyndall's theories, [b] even did they suffice to give a satisfactory explanation of the action of the geysers in Iceland, are assuredly totally inadequate to explain the action of all those of the Yellowstone Park. For the simple reason that the vapours escaping from some of them are so strongly impregnated with hydrochloric, sulphurous, and sulphuric acid gases, as well as with sulphuretted hydrogen, as to compel one to believe that chemical action plays a not unimportant part in the production of the phenomena there witnessed. Moreover, the solids brought up by the water closely resemble in chemical composition the lava ejected from burning mountains, inasmuch as, besides containing a large percentage of silica and alumina, they likewise consist of lime, potash, soda, magnesia, and iron, as well as of a small proportion of other metals, as was guessed at by the beautifully varied green, rose, yellow, and purple hues of the beds of the streamlets flowing from the craters of the geysers. The geysers of the Yellowstone, although situated at the height of 7765 feet above the level of the sea, nevertheless lie in valleys, for the mountains surrounding them are much higher still.

[b] Sir G. S. Mackenzie's 'Travels in Iceland,' in 1810, p. 228. Prof. Tyndall 'On Heat,' p. 126.

Some idea of the force with which the water issues from the earth, may be formed from the fact that it is in some cases sufficient to carry a column of over six feet in diameter 200 feet high, for the p. 160 space of twenty minutes at a time. And all know that 200 feet is nearly double the height of any ordinary church steeple. Moreover, the amount of solids brought up with the water may be imagined when I say that, in one of the boiling springs, the mixture so closely resembles thick milk gruel as to have given to it the name of the 'paint-pot,' and so loaded is its water with mineral matters, that they consolidate almost immediately after escaping from the spring's outlet. So thick indeed is it, that I kneaded some into the shape of a brick, which I have still in my possession. All the geyser water in this district is so charged with silicious earths that it consolidates sufficiently rapidly to form an upright rim around each geyser's vent. Just as a fringe of scoria and lava encircles the mouth of a burning mountain.

The rapidity with which the deposits form and solidify may be conjectured when I say that I saw trees growing close to some of the geysers whose stems and lower branches were so encrusted with geyserite as to give the idea that they were actually petrified. While again I saw an old horse shoe, which had only been fourteen days in the water, so completely enveloped with it that it looked exactly as if it had been hewn out of solid marble.

The mere glancing around, and noticing how the geysers had evidently, like human beings, but a transient existence, produced a somewhat strange sensation. For it was perfectly evident that they are born but to die. All of them appearing to spout p. 161 themselves permanently out. For while on one side some seemed just as if they were starting into existence, on another were those apparently in the very zenith of their strength, while others again looked as if they were making but their last feeble efforts at existence, though it was evident, from the heaps of consolidated geyserite surrounding them, that they had but recently passed through halcyon days of youthful energy and manhood power. Every here and there again we came upon others from whose wide open empty mouths came forth neither a puff of steam nor a drop of water. They were dead, and not a few of them were so completely eviscerated as to allow of the explorer to descend with perfect safety into the bowels of the earth through their vents. Geyser activity is in fact but the last act in the drama of volcanic life: all around proved this. Close at hand were stupendous cliffs of pure obsidian—the black bottle glass manufactured in Nature's furnaces. Even half a mile of our road was macadamised with it. And so similar not only in chemical composition but in optical properties is this obsidian to actual glass, that a flat piece I picked up on the road, just after it had been splintered off a block by one of the wheels of our carriage, is as transparent as any piece of black bottle glass of equal thickness. These mountains of obsidian plainly tell how awfully stupendous must have been the heating process which called them into existence, as well as how big must be the cavities left in the bowels p. 162 of the earth from which the materials constituting them were obtained. No doubt water scoops out caverns in the softer strata composing the earth's crust, but these can scarcely be thought to equal in extent the cavities made by volcanoes. Think, for example, of what a hole in the earth must have been left by the 50 miles long and 5 miles broad lava stream which flowed from Mauna Loa in 1859, and fell as a fiery cascade over a cliff into the sea, in sufficient amount to fill up a large bay.

The geyser basin is in many places actually honeycombed with various sized caverns, either directly due to volcanic action, or to water, or to both combined, and these caverns, though widely apart, may yet freely communicate with each other by means of subterranean river courses. I have myself followed one river course into the bowels of the earth for three miles and more, in the great Adelsberg Grotto, in Styria. I have rowed across the lake in the dismally dark cavern at Han, in the Ardennes. And even in our own Derbyshire, I have seen, half-a-mile from the entrance of the Speedwell Mine, a river, a water-fall, and a lake, all of which tell that such natural phenomena exist within the bowels of the earth as well as upon its surface. Moreover, the resounding echoes from the clatter of our horses' feet as they briskly trotted over some of the geyserite, as well as the heat we experienced through the thick leather soles of our boots as we walked across it, was unmistakable proof that but a thin layer of crust separated p. 163 the surface of the globe we were traversing in Wyoming and Montana not alone from vast caverns, but likewise from still active subterranean fires.

All the preceding facts I have narrated must be borne in mind, in order that the theory of geyser action I am now about to propound may be readily understood. For unless the reader believes:—

1st. That cavities of various shapes and sizes exist in the earth's crust;

2d. That the earth possesses internal lakes as well as rivers;

3d. That there are vast internal fires still actively at work in the neighbourhood of geysers; and,

4th. That the smell of the acid vapours and sulphuretted hydrogen, as well as the mineral matters dissolved and suspended in the ejected waters, are proof positive of chemical activity, he will entirely fail to perceive the value of my remarks regarding the cause of a geyser's action being not only spasmodic but periodic.

On the next page is an explanatory diagramatic sketch, in which no attempt has been made at the impossible, namely, to apportion the size, the shape, or the situation of the cavities to each other. As they may in reality be close together, or miles apart. They may all be on the same level, or more likely not. They may be of nearly equal dimensions, or of varying sizes. It matters not one whit, for the purposes of the demonstration of the theory of geyser action now being adduced. p. 164

a. A cavernous reservoir, receiving its water supply by streamlet feeders (*b*) from the hills (*a*). b. A natural, and, it may be, circuitous syphon conduit, by which the water can only reach chamber (c) after it has filled tube (b) to the level of the syphon's top, consequently the supply of water to chamber (c) is intermittent, and only lasts until the water in chamber (a) has sunk down to the orifice of its syphon connection. c. Is supposed to be the chemical laboratory in which the decomposable minerals are, and it is further supposed to be heated by subterranean fires. In case the reader knows but little of chemistry, I may remark that all chemical changes are greatly accelerated by heat, and that superheated steam is a most powerful agent in expediting the decomposition of earthy and alkaline compounds.

In the case of these subterranean laboratories, it is utterly impossible for even the scientifically trained mind to conceive what the extent of the heat may be. All he knows is that it is probably far greater than suffices to resolve water into its gaseous elements—oxygen and hydrogen—and that even before this point is reached, superheated steam becomes a terrifically formidable explosive agent. Look at what it did at Ban-dai-san in Japan last year. It actually split a mountain three miles in circumference in twain, and blew one half of it right away into a valley as if it had been the mere outside wall of a house. And such p. 165 was the force of the wind-shock it occasioned that all the trees growing on the opposite mountain's side were knocked down by it as if they had been mere nine-pins. (In 'Nature,' of the 17th January 1889, at p. 279, will be found an account of the scene of devastation when it was visited (in the month of October 1888) by my son Vaughan; the same who visited the geysers of the Yellowstone with me in 1884, and those of Iceland with his sister in 1887.)

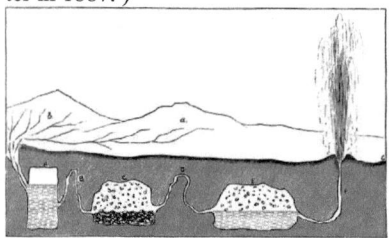

a. Water-tank. c. Chemical Laboratory. e. Geyser-water Reservoir. f. Geyser. *Page 164 .*

In the case of the geyser, superadded to the superheated steam's explosive power, there will be in addition that of the gases liberated by the decomposition of the carbonates, sulphates, and chlorides (under the combined influence of heat and water) in chamber (c), which I call for the nonce the chemical laboratory. Not alone will all earthy and alkaline, but even metallic compounds, like iron pyrites, therein contained, be rapidly decomposed on the advent of the superheated water. And from their gaseous elements being held in a confined space, they will acquire an enormous explosive power. Consequently, there is no difficulty in understanding how that on obtaining entrance into chamber (e) by means of conduit (d), they will instantly proceed to expel from it all its water. And from the water finding no other outlet except by vent (f), it will rush through it, and, by virtue of the propelling force of the gases, be thrown up into the air in the form of a geyser. Whose activity will only last so long as the supply of water in chamber (f) remains unexhausted. p. 166

The above being a rough outline of the salient points of what I consider to be a rational, though, it may be, incomplete, theory of the geyser action I saw in the Yellowstone Park, I shall now add a concluding word on the probable mode of action of the so-called 'earth-sod emetic' that my daughter describes as having been given to the 'Stroker' geyser in Iceland in order to make it eject its water.

The mode of action of the sods, I think, is easily enough explained on the supposition that the geyser has a constriction at some point or another in its vent, and that the sods plug it up sufficiently to hold back the steam and water until they have accumulated sufficient power to blow out the obstructing body, and escape after it with a rush into the air. Precisely in the same way as a fermenting barrel of beer blows out its bung, and its fluid contents gush out, when its vent-hole accidentally becomes plugged up.

George Harley, M.D., F.R.S.